DEDICATION

We dedicate this book to our good friends Mark Thiessen and Ron Barta. They encouraged us to write about the amazing attractions and places around our great state. We are grateful to have such wonderful friends.

1115

CONTENTS

Amusements and Entertainment

Sports and Recreation

Culture and History

Unique Attractions

PREFACE

For each of us, traveling has been an important part of our lives since we were young. Though Lisa isn't a native Nebraskan, the state played a major role in her childhood because her father hailed from Nebraska. The family visited almost annually, and each trip home required visits to Nebraska dining spots Runza, Little King, and Valentino's. Between Lincoln and Omaha, Lisa learned a lot about Nebraska growing up. Then a job opportunity brought her family to Omaha, which she's called home for more than thirty years.

As a native Nebraskan, Tim and his family moved a few times during his childhood. Calling Kennard, Oakland, and Fremont home, he traveled many parts of the state as a youth, including visiting his grandmother on the Santee Sioux Reservation in northeast Nebraska. One of his earliest travel memories is a family vacation to Minden's Pioneer Village. His travels also included visiting family in Arkansas, Georgia, and Montana.

As a couple, we've loved traveling together. Having both worked in the hospitality industry, we have enjoyed several chances to visit other cities and states. We love traveling Nebraska and experiencing events and attractions we heard about when we were younger, including crossing off Chimney Rock from our bucket lists. From NEBRASKAland Days in North Platte to the Winnebago powwow, we love exploring Nebraska.

When we hear visitors complain that Nebraska is flat, we smile and suggest that they get off the interstate. When they do, they'll find rolling hills and beautiful scenery, such as the Sandhills, Toadstool Geologic Park, and the Niobrara River. Small towns like Monowi—the smallest town in America—and Taylor invite people to get out of their cars and take a walk around town. Nebraska is home to great sports, such as the Nebraska and Creighton college programs, Omaha Storm Chasers baseball, and outstanding junior hockey.

As we created this book, we wanted to provide a balanced look at Nebraska, from the cities to the rural areas. We first created a list of items we were interested in sharing. It was difficult to pare it down to only a hundred, so if you don't see your hometown or favorite attraction, it's not an intentional slight. We wanted to share as much of the state as possible. We wanted to describe the state's "Good Life," as we know it—beautiful scenery, wonderful people, and great attractions and events. Travel the state and you'll see what we mean.

ACKNOWLEDGMENTS

We owe our families and friends a debt of gratitude for their support in our travel endeavors. For encouraging us to start *The Walking Tourists* travel blog, as well as supporting our work with two other books—*100 Things to Do in Omaha Before You Die* and *Unique Eats and Eateries of Omaha*—we truly appreciate their support.

Our families and careers led to us traveling the state and experiencing the "Good Life." From Lisa's dad instilling the travel bug in her early in life with job assignments that took the family around the country to her work in the hospitality industry, she has enjoyed the experiences she's encountered.

Tim mostly grew up in small towns and never dreamed of experiencing the travel opportunities he's had. From spending time in Europe while in the Air Force to traveling around the country to events such as the International Balloon Fiesta in Albuquerque, New Mexico, and Seafair in Seattle, Washington, he's enjoyed every opportunity. While visiting countries such as Northern Ireland and The Philippines were amazing travel experiences, Tim always appreciates coming home to Nebraska.

Thank you to everyone who has supported our adventures. We believe you'll enjoy this tour of Nebraska.

FOOD AND DRINK

1

ENJOY A BREW
AT A CLASSIC COFFEEHOUSE

Grab a hot cup of your favorite coffee, pull up a chair, and maybe read a book, surf the internet, or visit with friends. If you time it right, you can sit back and listen to eclectic music as the stage area of MiLady Coffee becomes Pioneer Theater. A popular spot since opening a couple of years ago, MiLady offers a unique coffeehouse experience in downtown Fremont. Calling the May Brothers Building home, MiLady takes its name from the coffee blend that wafted through the grocers' offices. MiLady also celebrates the frontier businessmen with a mural near the entrance showcasing a vintage photo of the men at work in the building during the early 1880s. In the afternoon, 1881 Pint Room joins MiLady on the first floor, offering Nebraska-brewed beers and wines.

105 E. Sixth St., Fremont, NE 68025
(402) 206-2125, facebook.com/miladycoffeehouse

FUN FACT

Fremont, Nebraska, residents Luther H. Griffith and Edward Blewett later traveled west and founded Fremont, Washington. The Seattle neighborhood is known for its eclectic attractions, such as a statue of Soviet leader Vladimir Lenin and a troll made from sand that lives under a bridge.

Hardy Coffee Co.
2112 N. Thirtieth St.
Omaha, NE 68111
(402) 505-9685
hardycoffee.com

The Chocolate Bar
116 W. Third St.
Grand Island, NE 68801
(308) 675-0664
thechocolatebargi.com

Scooter's Coffee
1550 Harlan Dr.
Bellevue, NE 68005
(402) 932-5665
scooterscoffee.com

The Mill Coffee & Tea
800 P St., Lincoln, NE 68508
(402) 475-5522
millcoffee.com

Brew Coffeehouse and Tasting Room
318 N. Spruce St.
Valley, NE 68064
(402) 933-7255
brewcoffeevalley.com

Roast Coffeehouse
1904 S. Sixty-Seventh St.
Omaha, NE 68106
(402) 991-2326
ahillofbeans.com

Legend Comics and Coffee
5207 Leavenworth St.
Omaha, NE 68106
(402) 391-2377
legendcomicsandcoffee.com

The Beanery
344 S. Washington St.
Papillion, NE 68046
(402) 991-1649
thebeanerycoffee.com

Mo Java Café
2649 N. Forty-Eighth St.
Lincoln, NE 68504
(402) 464-4130, mojava.net

Dakota Perk
3900 Dakota Ave.
South Sioux City, NE 68776
(402) 404-8080
dakotaperk.com

Gotta Get Some Coffee
621 S. Thirteenth St.
Tekamah, NE 68061
(402) 658-2365, facebook.
com/pg/gottagetsomecoffee

The Downtown Coffee Company and Bistro
302 Norfolk Ave.
Norfolk, NE 68701
(402) 844-3699
downtowncoffee.co

2

UNWRAP DELICIOUSNESS
AT BAKERS CANDIES

Bakers Candies is the largest candy outlet in Nebraska at more than six thousand square feet, so chocolate lovers risk overdoing it when shopping for some of the best candy in the Cornhusker State. Founded more than thirty years ago, the family-owned Greenwood company originally sold chocolates and candy at its factory store. Then, in 2019, Bakers added the outlet next door. Known for its foil-wrapped meltaways—because they melt in your mouth—Bakers produces more than thirty million pieces annually. With flavors such as cherry, orange, mint, raspberry, and coconut, it's difficult to find a favorite. They can be shipped to every state in the union and are especially popular during holidays such as Christmas and Valentine's Day. While people enjoy visiting the outlet store, Bakers Candies can also be purchased in Omaha and Lincoln, as well as online. Bakers also produces candies such as spice drops, cinnamon treats, and chocolate-covered marshmallows.

831 S. Baker St., Greenwood, NE 68366
(402) 789-2700, bakerscandies.com

Licorice International in Lincoln's Haymarket District is another unique Nebraska sweet shop. Offering licorice and other candies from around the world, Licorice International stocks flavors such as green apple, cinnamon, strawberry, and root beer. The shop is a popular stop in the historic district.

3

THANK DOROTHY LYNCH
FOR LEADING NEBRASKANS TO SALAD

Who knew that a little old salad dressing created inside the American Legion in St. Paul would become a staple in restaurants and homes from Omaha to Sidney? Art and Dorothy Lynch were running the Legion's kitchen when she created the tomato-based dressing in the late 1940s. Sweet and spicy, the salad dressing quickly became popular with diners. After the Lynches began bottling and selling the dressing as Dorothy Lynch Home Style Dressing, sales spread like wildfire. By the mid-1960s, they couldn't keep up with demand and sold the recipe to a Columbus-based company. Today, Tasty Toppings produces millions of bottles of Dorothy Lynch at its Duncan plant, shipping to stores and restaurants around the country. With Tasty Toppings' headquarters at Dusters, the Columbus restaurant is considered the home of Dorothy Lynch. A visit to Dusters offers guests great food, such as steaks and burgers. But every meal starts with salad topped by Dorothy Lynch.

Dusters
2804 Thirteenth St., Columbus, NE 68601
(402) 564-8338, dustersrestaurant.com

Dorothy Lynch/Tasty Toppings
2804 Thirteenth St., Columbus, NE 68601
(402) 564-1347, dorothylynch.com

People use tasty Dorothy Lynch dressing in all types of dishes, from little smoky sausages prepared in a Dorothy Lynch marinade to chicken wings coated with the dressing. Nebraskans are also known to use the sweet and spicy dressing in chili.

4

ENJOY A STEAK
AT A CLASSIC STEAKHOUSE

Nebraska ranks as one of the top beef producers in the United States, shipping corn-fed steaks around the country, as well as internationally to nations such as Japan. With T-bones, strips, and rib eyes leading the way, you can enjoy a steak dinner at any of Nebraska's classic steakhouses. Johnny's Café in South Omaha will celebrate its centennial birthday in 2022. Originally located near the Omaha Stockyards, Johnny's catered to ranchers, farmers, and businessmen alike. Today, with the stockyards an Omaha memory, Johnny's Café continues to serve outstanding steak. In western Nebraska, people savor hand-cut steaks at Peppermill Restaurant in Valentine. Considered among the best restaurants in the state, Peppermill ages its top steak—the Mulligan—for seven to ten weeks. Popular with locals, visitors, and celebrities alike, Misty's Steakhouse and Lounge in Lincoln scores as many points with its fans as the nearby Huskers football team. Known for its prime rib, Misty's also serves outstanding steaks.

DID YOU KNOW?

Nebraska ranks second in cattle production in the United States. Nebraska, Texas, and Kansas together account for almost a third of the cattle raised in the country.

Johnny's Café
4702 S. Twenty-Seventh St.
Omaha, NE 68107
(402) 731-4774
johnnyscafe.com

Peppermill Restaurant
502 E. Hwy. 20
Valentine, NE 69201
(402) 376-2800
peppermillvalentine.com

Misty's Steakhouse and Lounge
6235 Havelock Ave.
Lincoln, NE 68507
(402) 466-8424
mistyslincoln.com

Omaha Prime
415 S. Eleventh St.
Omaha, NE 68102
(402) 341-7040
omaha-prime.com

Cascio's Steakhouse
1620 S. Tenth St.
Omaha, NE 68108
(402) 345-8313
casciossteakhouse.com

Plainsman Steakhouse and Lounge
103 E. Fourteenth St.
Juniata, NE 68955
(402) 751-2512
the-plainsman.com/pm

The Drover
Omaha, NE 68124
(402) 391-7440
droverrestaurant.com

The Office Bar and Grill
121 N. Main St.
Hooper, NE 68031
(402) 654-3373
officebarandgrill.net

Round the Bend Steakhouse
30801 E. Park Hwy.
Ashland, NE 68003
(402) 944-9974
roundthebendsteakhouse.com

Gorat's
4917 Center St.
Omaha, NE 68106
(402) 551-3733
goratsomaha.com

Anthony's Steakhouse
7220 F St., Omaha, NE 68127
(402) 331-7575
anthonyssteakhouse.com

Farmer Brown's Steakhouse
2620 River Road Dr.
Waterloo, NE 68069
(402) 779-2353
farmerbrowns.com

Brother Sebastian's Steak House and Winery
1350 S. 119th St.
Omaha, NE 68144
(402) 330-0300
brothersebastians.com

5

ENJOY A SWEET TREAT
AT SPRINGFIELD'S SODA FOUNTAIN

The soda fountain jerk serves up a tall one and listens to all your problems. Oops, wrong place. At Springfield Drug's soda fountain, you'll enjoy ice cream treats, such as malts and banana splits, or even phosphate drinks. Located on a corner in the small Sarpy County town, Springfield Drug has helped people since the late 1970s. A true small-town pharmacy, in addition to filling prescriptions, it sells all kinds of goods, such as greeting cards and household supplies. While you enjoy an ice cream treat, browse the store and view some of the unique antiques calling the pharmacy home. While you're in Springfield Drug, you'll also need to take a picture with the *Simpsons* cartoon characters, who occupy a bench inside the store. The building was once a bank, so you may even see the vault. The Springfield Drug soda fountain is one of only a few left in Nebraska.

205 Main St., Springfield, NE 68059
(402) 253-2000, facebook.com/SpringfieldOldFashionedSoda

FUN FACT

For more than eighty years, Springfield has been home to the Sarpy County Fair. Each year in early August, thousands of people visit the fair, home to 4-H livestock and agriculture competitions, carnival rides, and food on a stick. Cowboys participate in the nightly rodeo, seeking prizes for bronco busting, bull riding, and more.

ENJOY A DRINK WITH HISTORY
AT GLUR'S TAVERN

From celebrities to politicians, Glur's Tavern in Columbus has seen it all since opening in 1876. Count cowboy showman Buffalo Bill Cody among its many guests. It's said that Buffalo Bill and his entourage visited Bucher's Saloon (its original name) whenever they traveled through the area. Nebraska politicians make it a key campaign stop to shake hands and maybe enjoy a drink with voters. As Glur's continues as the oldest continually operating tavern west of the Mississippi River, it caters to locals, who are known to bring their families along for a burger. Louis Glur changed the name of the saloon, which is listed on the National Register of Historic Places, in the early 1900s after he bought the establishment from William Bucher. Glur's Tavern stayed in the family until the late 1970s. Today the tavern both entertains locals and attracts visitors who want to see the historic bar.

2301 Eleventh St., Columbus, NE 68601
(402) 564-8615, facebook.com/Glurs-Tavern-114094411990524

7

RECOGNIZE HISTORY
AT LINCOLN'S HAYMARKET DISTRICT

In Lincoln's early days, the town's economy flowed through the market square. Farmers and ranchers brought their produce and livestock to the market near Salt Creek. Later, the federal government built a post office in the area, pushing the market a couple of blocks north, where it became the Haymarket. Today the legacy continues as the Haymarket Landmark District. Consisting of an eight-block area in the old warehouse district, it is home to restaurants, bars, shops, and coffeehouses. During the day, families roam the Haymarket, spending time in shops such as Licorice International and Flatwater Toys, as well as the Bill Harris Iron Horse Park, home to a 3-D mural on the former Burlington Northern Railroad depot. At night, the scene gives way to people seeking a nice dinner at restaurants such as Buzzard Billy's or Leadbelly, or visiting bars and clubs such as Barry's Bar and Grill, the Starlite Lounge, and Kinkaider Brewing Co.

lincolnhaymarket.org

FUN FACT

Next door to the Haymarket, the Railyard opened in 2013 as a restaurant and entertainment district. A little more contemporary than the Haymarket, the Railyard offers seasonal attractions. During the fall, hundreds of people gather to watch Nebraska football games on a big-screen television known as the Cube. In winter, the spot becomes an ice-skating rink. The University of Nebraska men's and women's basketball teams play at Pinnacle Bank Arena, located on the northern edge of the Railyard.

8

ENJOY THE SCENERY AND A DRINK

AT JAMES ARTHUR VINEYARDS

Driving through Nebraska's countryside, you're used to seeing fields with corn seemingly growing a mile high and soybeans that change color toward harvesttime. Then you notice vines wrapping themselves around posts a few feet above the ground. Look more closely and you'll see green and purple grapes reaching their own harvest colors. With almost thirty wineries and more than two hundred vineyards around the state, Nebraska's wine industry has experienced tremendous growth over the past three decades. James Arthur Vineyards near Raymond ranks among the best known of the wineries. With ten varieties of grapes grown over twenty acres to create award-winning wines, such as its Edelweiss and Two Brothers, James Arthur Vineyards provides a memorable experience. Enjoy a glass of red or white and a charcuterie plate on the patio and then explore the grounds, including a walk through the vineyard.

2001 W. Raymond Rd., Raymond, NE 68428
(402) 783-5255, jamesarthurvineyards.com

Cuthills Vineyard
54663 853rd Rd.
Pierce, NE 68767
(402) 329-6774
facebook.com/pages/Cuthills-Vineyard/253182564722711

Soaring Wings Vineyard and Brewing
17111 S. 138th St.
Springfield, NE 68059
(402) 253-2479
soaringwingswine.com

Nissen Wine
88973 Hwy. 57
Hartington, NE 68739
(402) 254-3426
nissenwine.com

Glacial Till Vineyard
344 S. Second Rd.
Palmyra, NE 68418
(402) 610-3068
glacialtillvineyard.com

Mac's Creek Winery and Brewery
43315 Rd. 757
Lexington, NE 68850
(308) 324-0440
macscreek.com

Niobrara Valley Vineyards
90256 State Spur 16F
Nenzel, NE 69219
(402) 823-4131
nvvsandhills.com

Big Cottonwood Vineyards and Winery
2865 County Rd. I
Tekamah, NE 68061
(402) 374-2656
bigcottonwoodwinery.com

Silver Hills Vineyard and Winery
3130 County Rd. M
Tekamah, NE 68061
(402) 374-1602
silverhillswinery.com

Feather River Vineyards
5700 E. State Farm Rd.
North Platte, NE 69101
(308) 696-0078
feather-river.com

Superior Estates Winery
200 W. Fifteenth St.
Superior, NE 68978
(402) 879-3001
superiorestateswinery.com

Schilling Bridge Winery
62193 710th Rd.
Pawnee City, NE 68420
(402) 852-2400
schillingbridgewinery.com

Miletta Vista Winery
1732 Hwy. 281
St. Paul, NE 68873
(308) 754-4416
milettavistawinery.com

9

SAY CHEESE
AT JISA'S FARMSTEAD CHEESE

Wisconsin may be known as the dairy state, but don't tell Dave Jisa. The Brainard dairy farmer sought a new revenue stream when milk prices dropped in the early 2000s. After learning how to make cheese, the Nebraskan turned his three-hundred-cow dairy farm into a cheese producer. Jisa's operation started producing the delectable dairy staple in 2005. How well did the Brainard operation do? Eight years after opening, Jisa took his cheese curds to the Land of the Curds—Wisconsin. Going head to head with the upper Midwestern cheeseheads, Jisa's New York Cheese Curds took third place honors at the American Cheese Society's competition. Using natural processes to create cheese, Jisa's farm provides all its own resources. Jisa refuses to sacrifice quality, and Jisa Farmstead Cheese now offers almost two dozen flavors that can be found in stores around the state or at the Jisa farmstead store.

2653 Q Rd., Brainard, NE 68626
(402) 545-2000, jisacheese.com

10

DINE WITH THE BIG GAME

AT OLE'S

Come to Ole's Big Game Steakhouse and Lounge for the food. Stay for the two hundred big game trophies and taxidermized animals. The steakhouse in small-town Paxton is a major attraction for anyone traveling in the Sandhills. It has been open since 1933, and steakhouse diners are usually amazed by the trophy busts of exotic animals such as elephants, giraffes, bighorn sheep, and baboons. There's even a large taxidermized polar bear from Russia near the entrance. It started with a whitetail buck, and Ole added to the collection for more than thirty years. The trophies come from all over the world, including England, Central America, and Canada. But Ole's is about more than the big game trophies. It is home to some of the best steak in Nebraska, and you can also grab a burger or chicken dinner. Ole's is a short drive off I-80 and is located along US 30, also known as the Lincoln Highway.

123 N. Oak St., Paxton, NE 69155
(308) 239-4500, olesbiggame.com

11

ENJOY A CRAFT BREW
AT KINKAIDER BREWING CO.

With beer names such as Devil's Gap and Moscow Mule, Kinkaider Brewing Co. isn't your grandparents' brewery. Or even your parents'. Born from home brewing, the upstart brewery continues to catch fire around Nebraska as it delivers its unique and fun beers from small-town Broken Bow to bars and taprooms in Lincoln, Omaha, Grand Island, and places in between. Its founders first excelled at creating home brews. A friend—who later became a partner—told them their beer was better than anything he bought. So the three of them decided to look for a place to open a brewery. A pumpkin patch near town proved the perfect spot, and the patch's owner became the fourth partner. Since 2015, the four have produced outstanding craft beer using local crops such as pumpkins and jalapeños. The team honored their ancestors by taking their name from the Kinkaid Act, which sought to recruit settlers to Nebraska's Sandhills.

43860 Paulsen Rd., Broken Bow, NE 68822
(308) 872-8348, kinkaiderbrewing.com

DID YOU KNOW?

Craft brewing in Nebraska is a growing industry. With about fifty breweries, the state has seen local beer sales more than triple since 2010, from more than 482,000 gallons to almost 1.5 million.

Kros Strain Brewing Co.
10411 Portal Rd.
La Vista, NE 68128
(402) 779-7990
krosstrainbrewing.com

Pint Nine Brewing Co.
10411 Portal Rd., Ste. 104
Papillion, NE 68128
(402) 359-1418
pintninebrewing.com

Nebraska Brewing Co.
6950 S. 108th St.
La Vista, NE 68128
(402) 934-7988
nebraskabrewingco.com

Pals Brewing Co.
4520 S. Buffalo Bill Ave.
North Platte, NE 69101
(308) 221-6715
palsbrewingcompany.com

Thunderhead Brewing Co.
18 E. Twenty-First St.
Kearney, NE 68847
(308) 237-1558
thunderheadbrewing.com

Scratchtown Brewing Co.
141 S. Sixteenth St.
Ord, NE 68862
(308) 728-5050
scratchtown.beer

Loop Brewing Co.
404 W. A St.
McCook, NE 69001
(308) 345-5198
loopbrewingcompany.com

Zipline Brewing Co.
2100 Magnum Cir., Ste. 1
Lincoln, NE 68522
(402) 475-1001
ziplinebrewing.com

Empyrean Brewing Co.
729 Q St.
Lincoln, NE 68508
(402) 434-5960
empyreanbrewingco.com

Vis Major Brewing Co.
3501 Center St.
Omaha, NE 68105
(402) 884-4082
vismajorbrewing.com

Divots Brewery
4200 W. Norfolk Ave.
Norfolk, NE 68701
(402) 844-2981
divotsbrewery.com

Lucky Bucket Brewing Co.
11941 Centennial Rd., Ste. 1
La Vista, NE 68128
(402) 763-8868
luckybucket.beer

12

TAKE A BITE OF AN APPLE ORCHARD
IN NEBRASKA CITY

Nebraska City has long been considered *the* place to pick apples in Nebraska. A visit to Arbor Day Farm is more than a trip to pick apples. You can visit a fifty-foot-tall treehouse atop a tree trail, which features opportunities to see nature exhibits along the way. Walk among the canopy of treetops as you visit Tree Top Village, a set of eleven small treehouses connected through a series of rope bridges. At the end, ride the slide fifty feet to the ground. Arbor Day Farm also features a hiking trail with several attractions, such as giant chairs and gnome homes. Don't forget to pick your apples before leaving.

At Kimmel Orchard and Vineyard, you can enjoy a nature hike along the Tree Dome Trail, featuring native plants and animal tracks for children to identify. Afterward, have fun picking your own apples from the orchard.

Union Orchard grows about twenty varieties of apples, and visitors can enjoy a ride to the orchard in a covered wagon.

FUN FACT

The third weekend of September turns all apple in Nebraska City as the community celebrates the AppleJack Festival. More than seventy thousand people visit over a three-day period, taking in activities, exhibits, and a major parade.

Arbor Day Farm
2611 Arbor Ave., Nebraska City, NE 68410
(402) 873-8717, arbordayfarm.org

Kimmel Orchard and Vineyard
5995 G Rd., Nebraska City, NE 68410
(402) 873-5293, kimmelorchard.org

Wostrel Family's Union Orchard
2405 S. Hwy. 75, Union, NE 68455
(402) 263-4845, unionorchard.com

13

TASTE A NEBRASKA ORIGINAL

WITH A RUNZA

If you ask a Nebraskan for one food you should try, an overwhelming majority will respond with a Runza. The popular sandwich shares its name with the restaurant. Uniquely Nebraskan, a Runza consists of a freshly baked bread pocket filled with seasoned ground beef, chopped onions, and cabbage. It is based on a German-Russian dish. The first Runza restaurant opened in Lincoln in 1949. Now more than eighty Runza restaurants are located throughout Nebraska, Colorado, Iowa, and Kansas. They're even sold at University of Nebraska football games. Customers don't just live for a Runza; they also love the crisp crinkle fries and handmade onion rings. True Runzatics order frings, a combination of fries and onion rings. Oh, and from fall through spring, you can warm your insides with a delicious bowl of chili and a side of cinnamon rolls, another Husker State original.

Multiple locations
runza.com

DID YOU KNOW?

Nebraskans love Runza so much that people who have moved out of state crave it and make it one of their first stops when they return home.

SKIP THE PASSWORD, ENJOY THE STEAK

AT THE SPEAKEASY

You don't need a password for this speakeasy. You'll wish you did, though, to keep the place to yourself. You might expect to find a place like The Speakeasy in Sacramento, California, instead of Sacramento, Nebraska. Actually, it's a restaurant you're more likely to visit in a city like Omaha, Kansas City, or Chicago—you know, people who know steak. Instead of heading to the big city, Ryan Puls took over the family steakhouse from his dad a few years ago and created an eatery that attracts people from Omaha, Kansas City, and Chicago. Located at the end of a gravel road in a true ghost town (ask about Faceless Fred), The Speakeasy takes you to a special place, gastronomically speaking. Start with the house-cured, smoked pork belly, a delicacy Puls perfected while cooking in Seattle. Then order a steak (on weekends, get the slow-roasted version) and enjoy the perfectly charred exterior and succulent center.

72993 S Rd., Sacramento, NE 68949
(308) 995-4757, thespeakeasyrestaurant.com

15

TAKE THE STELLANATOR CHALLENGE

AT STELLA'S

Your mission, should you choose to accept it, is to down six burger patties, twelve bacon slices, six cheese slices, six fried eggs, a bun, a ton of toppings, and a side of French fries—all within forty-five minutes. If you manage that, the Stellanator is free, and you get a t-shirt and your name on the wall of fame. Many have tried to complete the Stellanator challenge at Stella's Bar and Grill in Bellevue, but few succeed. (They end up paying thirty-five dollars for the massive burger.) Molly Schuyler, a competitive eater, has devoured the Stellanator in three minutes and forty seconds. But most diners stay far away from the challenge, settling for a single patty with unique toppings such as peanut butter and bacon or fried egg and jalapeño, whatever your little heart desires. Stella's opened in 1936, and its burgers have been named the best in Omaha for nearly a decade.

106 S. Galvin Rd., Bellevue, NE 68005
(402) 291-6088, stellasbarandgrill.com

16

CHEW THE BULL
AT ASHLAND'S TESTICLE FESTIVAL

Only in Nebraska can you attract thousands of people to eat Rocky Mountain oysters—bull testicles. While festivalgoers debate whether the definition of Rocky Mountain oysters applies to bulls or pigs, one thing is certain: people enjoy tasting the breaded treats. Round the Bend Steakhouse—the sponsor of the annual event—serves about two tons of sliced testicles over a two-day period each Father's Day weekend. The event features live music and other entertainment, and people attend from all over the Midwest. With fans cheering on participants, the festival also hosts a ball-eating contest. Unlike some testicle festivals that can get rowdy and violent, Ashland's Testicle Festival is a family-friendly event. As it nears its thirtieth year, the Testicle Festival has grown from a few hundred people in the early 1990s to nearly four thousand at recent events.

30801 E. Park Hwy., Ashland, NE 68003
(402) 994-9974, roundthebendsteakhouse.com

17

SAMPLE THE SWEETS
AT MASTER'S HAND

Since first making homemade candles as a fundraiser nearly twenty years ago, Susie Robison has created one of eastern Nebraska's most popular boutique shops. Master's Hand Candle Co. and Gift Shop is also home to Serendipity Chocolate Factory, featuring handmade chocolate treats, such as large, juicy chocolate-covered strawberries. The boutique has also grown to include a tea room, which serves breakfast and lunch. The store stocks home decor and accessories based on the seasons, with Christmas and Valentine's Day among its most popular holidays. As Master's Hand has grown in popularity, Susie has added community events, including the annual Spring Fling egg hunt, which has been coined "the biggest Easter egg hunt west of the Mississippi," featuring about twelve hundred plastic eggs filled with prizes. The event attracts thousands of people from as far away as Illinois. Susie, whose late husband Scott was her business partner, also owns side businesses, including a chipped ice wagon.

3599 County Rd. F, Tekamah, NE 68061
(402) 374-2003, mastershandcandles.com

LEARN ABOUT TEKAMAH AND BURT COUNTY HISTORY

As the county seat of Burt County, Tekamah is also home to the Burt County Museum. Located inside the former E. C. Houston mansion, the museum is a collection of items donated by area residents to honor families and to tell the story of the county's residents. With artifacts such as oil-powered clothes irons, antique kitchen utensils, and vintage clothing, the museum offers an interesting look into the area's history.

GREAT
AMERICAN
Wild West
SHOW

AMUSEMENTS AND ENTERTAINMENT

PLAY COWBOY
AT NEBRASKALAND DAYS

For ten days every June, thousands visit North Platte, the hometown of Buffalo Bill Cody, to play cowboy . . . or at least take part in one of the largest public celebrations in the Midwest. NEBRASKAland Days features a four-day professional rodeo, a carnival, and concerts featuring some of the nation's best-known country music performers. While some people try to win stuffed animals at midway games, such as tossing rings over empty soda bottles or using a sledgehammer to test their strength, others enjoy testing their willpower on thrill rides or relaxing on the Ferris wheel.

With a community parade to kick off the celebration, NEBRASKAland Days includes several events, such as an antique car show and mutton busting, all leading up to the rodeo, which is sanctioned by the Professional Rodeo Cowboys Association. The rodeo features some of the best cowboys and cowgirls in the nation.

NEBRASKAland Days closes with concerts featuring country acts such as Lady Antebellum, Florida Georgia Line, and Toby Keith.

2801 Charlie Evans Dr., North Platte, NE 69101
(308) 532-7939, nebraskalanddays.com

Buffalo Bill Cody, who chose to live on a ranch in North Platte when he retired, created the first "Wild West Show" in 1882 when the city didn't have any July Fourth celebration plans. He later hosted another show in Omaha before eventually taking his act around the country and later to Europe.

19

ENJOY THE SHOW
AT OMAHA'S HISTORICAL ORPHEUM THEATER

From vaudeville acts to Broadway-style productions, the Orpheum Theater in Omaha has continued to thrive since opening in 1927. The theater actually closed for a few years in 1971 after serving as a movie theater, with its last showing being Disney's *The Barefoot Executive*. It stood empty for about four years, until the Aksarben Foundation bought and renovated the building in 1975. It eventually donated the theater to the city of Omaha. Since then, the Orpheum has hosted live performances, including comedy acts and concerts. But it's now best known for hosting Broadway-quality shows, with *Wicked* remaining one of the all-time favorite musicals. In fact, the theater has a special trap door on stage known as the Wicked door because the show performs there so often. The theater has undergone many renovations over the past forty years, including changing the iconic outdoor sign from light bulbs to LED lighting.

409 S. Sixteenth St., Omaha, NE 68102
(402) 661-8501, omahaperformingarts.org

DID YOU KNOW?

The Orpheum Theater's Broadway productions are of such great quality that people have been known to fly into Omaha to catch a show rather than travel to New York to see it on Broadway.

Omaha-Area Theaters

The Rose
2001 Farnam St., Omaha, NE 68102
(402) 345-4849, rosetheater.org

Omaha Community Playhouse
6915 Cass St., Omaha, NE 68132
(402) 553-0800, omahaplayhouse.com

BLUEBARN Theatre
1106 S. Tenth St., Omaha, NE 68108
(402) 345-1576, bluebarn.org

20

CELEBRATE NEBRASKA
AT THE STATE FAIR

For eleven days each August, Grand Island becomes Ground Zero as the Nebraska State Fair celebrates all things Nebraska. From livestock competitions to food on a stick, the event attracts more than three hundred thousand people. While carnival rides and food may be the biggest draws, fairgoers also enjoy concerts that feature major acts, as well as classic favorites. With expectations including, well, almost anything on a stick, fairgoers are likely to find unique fair foods such as Philly cheesesteaks and mac 'n' cheese hamburgers. Seeking a state fair championship ribbon, youths from around the state bring their county fair-winning livestock to Grand Island. You'll see them primping their animals to look perfect for the judges. Prior to moving to Grand Island in 2010, the state fair was held in Lincoln. Nebraska has celebrated the state fair for more than 150 years.

501 E. Fonner Park Rd., Grand Island, NE 68801
(308) 382-1620, statefair.org

21

GET YOUR CLUCK ON

AT THE WAYNE CHICKEN SHOW

Only in Nebraska does a town build a weekend festival around chickens. And, boy, does Wayne pull it off. The three-day event each July focuses on all things chicken, from a cluck-off where people compete to sound the most like a chicken (yes, it's a thing) to a boiled-egg-eating contest. A chicken parade takes place on Saturday, and a petting zoo features all kinds of animals, not just chickens. Because the weekend highlights the fun aspects of chickens—such as their mannerisms and clucking—you can expect to see people wearing chicken hats, beaks, and feet. Locals created the festival more than forty years ago when they wanted something fresh to attract people to Wayne. Their thinking was that chickens are fun, everyone knows them, and they can inspire fun art projects. At the Wayne Chicken Show, you'll now find plenty of arts and crafts, as well as a car show and fireworks display.

(402) 375-2240, chickenshow.com

FIND THE GREAT PUMPKIN AND MORE
AT VALA'S PUMPKIN PATCH

Nicknamed Nebraska's Disneyland, Vala's Pumpkin Patch and Apple Orchard grew from a small pumpkin patch to a major tourist attraction over thirty years. While thousands of people flock to the Gretna farm each fall to pick out the perfect pumpkin, they also take in rides, shows, haunted houses, and more. While you're there, check out the pumpkin-eating dragon, get lost in Vala's corn maze, and enjoy a wagon ride to the field to harvest your own giant pumpkin to carve. You can also grab a handful of treats and head to the petting zoo or root for swine at the pig races. Children love playing on the bouncing pads or riding the train around the farm's apple orchard. On your way out, stop by the general store and purchase a few homemade treats, such as kettle corn, caramel apples, and a plethora of pumpkin and apple delights.

12102 S. 180th St., Gretna, NE 68028
(402) 332-4200, valaspumpkinpatch.com

The Steel And Foam Energy Reduction (SAFER) Barrier
Big Car Racing
Wooden Rails and Rooster Tails
500
May 30th 1934
CHAMPION
linkite
ELEK-TEK
Computer Wonderland
TEAM BLUEPRINT
The Dragster Guys!
27
CAR CRAFTERS
Collision Center
BLUEPRINT
PENNZOIL
Firestone
Firestone
Firestone

SPORTS AND RECREATION

23

ROAM THE WILD
AT THE LEE SIMMONS CONSERVATION PARK

Considered one of the best wildlife parks in the United States, the Lee G. Simmons Conservation Park and Wildlife Safari near Ashland offers a unique look into the lives of animals such as elk, bison, white-tailed deer, and black bears. A four-mile drive takes you along gravel roads, with an opportunity to get up close to the animals. They may even walk next to your vehicle (but never touch them, as they are wild animals). A popular destination, the wetlands offer a look at the lives of pelicans. Unable to fly because of injuries, these white birds spend their time swimming in a lagoon and diving for fish and other water treasures. You'll also see them waddle along the road flapping their wings. The Hands-on Corral offers children of all ages an opportunity to pet pygmy goats, chickens, and other farm animals. While there, hop on the old tractor.

16406 N. 292nd St., Ashland, NE 68003
(402) 944-9453, wildlifesafaripark.com

DID YOU KNOW?

The Simmons Conservation Park is a sister attraction to Omaha's Henry Doorly Zoo & Aquarium. In addition to the animals on display, the park houses animals from the zoo and serves as part of the zoo's conservation program.

24

TAKE A WALK ACROSS THE MISSOURI RIVER
ON THE BOB

Standing guard, OMAR the Troll greets you as you cross the Missouri River from Omaha to Council Bluffs on the Bob Kerrey Pedestrian Bridge. The longest pedestrian bridge to connect two states, the Bob ranks as one of the most popular attractions in Omaha. People love taking pictures of their feet standing in two states where Nebraska and Iowa meet midway across the river. Anchoring the riverfront, the three thousand foot-long bridge opened in 2008. Since then, the area has enjoyed tremendous growth, with the Lewis and Clark Landing hosting several local festivals, including Taste of Omaha and the SeptemberFest celebration of labor. Just north sits the River City Star, a paddleboat that conducts tours along the river.

705 Riverfront Dr., Omaha, NE 68102
visitomaha.com/bob

FUN FACT

Bob's bridge design reflects the flow of the Missouri River. You can learn more about the river's history and people's reliance on it through a display at the National Park Service's Midwest office near the foot of the bridge.

25

EXPLORE THE PLATTE
WITH BRYSON'S AIRBOAT TOURS

From pioneers crossing the Platte River in the 1800s to people kayaking there today, the Platte River has played many roles. But the best way to have fun on the river involves riding an air boat as it skims across sandbars peeking above the shallow water. A trip along the river with Bryson's Airboat Tours in Fremont offers more than a ride; it creates lasting memories. Cruising along the river, you'll feel the breeze in your face as you seemingly travel at the speed of sound (the boat actually travels at about twenty miles per hour). With outings from one to three hours, an airboat excursion provides views of the Platte River you don't usually see from the road, including eagles soaring above the trees and herons wading in the water. As you move farther upriver, you'll discover bluffs rising high above you. Longer outings also include a barbecue and sand volleyball.

839 County Rd. 19, Fremont, NE 68025
(402) 968-8534, brysonsairboattours.com

Fremont Attractions

Fremont Lakes State Recreation Area

Home to camping, swimming, and fishing, the Fremont state lakes, as locals call them, are a popular destination for outdoor enthusiasts. Located a few miles west of the city, the recreation area consists of twenty sandpit lakes.

4349 W. State Lakes Rd., Fremont, NE 68025

(402) 727-2922, outdoornebraska.gov/fremontlakes

Fremont Antique Stores

Downtown Fremont is home to more than half a dozen antique shops. With items ranging from vintage magazines and cookbooks to furniture and home decor, Fremont's antique stores are a downtown adventure.

visitfremontne.org/play/antiques

Louis E. May Museum

Offering a look at Fremont's history, the Louis E. May Museum on Nye Avenue is located in one of the city's first mansions and offers a beautiful garden.

1643 N. Nye Ave., Fremont, NE 68025

(402) 721-4515, maymuseum.com

RIDE 'EM COWBOY
AT THE BURWELL RODEO

For kids who dream of growing up to be cowboys, the Burwell rodeo may be the icing on the cake. Started by the small Central Nebraska town nearly a century ago, the Burwell rodeo—Nebraska's Big Rodeo—attracts more than ten thousand fans annually. More than four hundred cowpokes participate in events such as bronc busting, bull roping, and barrel racing. Entertainment includes chuckwagon races and rodeo clown acts. The Professional Rodeo Cowboys Association has recognized Burwell as one of the best rodeos in the country. Garfield County hosts its annual fair alongside Nebraska's Big Rodeo, creating a week-long event that includes 4-H livestock shows, carnival rides, and a parade. The community also hosts the Nebraska Little Rodeo, which focuses on children's events such as sheep riding, steer riding, and a calf scramble.

46710 L St., Burwell, NE 68823
(308) 346-5010, nebraskasbigrodeo.com

FUN FACT

Burwell is home to the annual Nebraska Prairie Chicken Festival, held each April. Thousands of people visit the town to watch colorful prairie chickens dance and sing during their mating season. The festival strives to educate visitors on their rituals and the significance of prairie chickens to the area.

KAYAK
THE SCENIC NIOBRARA RIVER

There may be no better spot to enjoy Nebraska's beautiful scenery than from a kayak cruising along the Niobrara River. With a slow-moving current, the Niobrara is perfect for enjoying a sunny summer day on the water. You'll appreciate impressive views of cliffs and waterfalls as you explore the river on a self-guided trip or join others on an outfitter-led float. It's recommended for novices to take the river along the Niobrara National Scenic River from Berry Bridge to Rocky Ford. Beyond that point, you'll want to be a more skillful kayaker, as you'll encounter class two rapids downriver. Spending the day on the Niobrara also means exploring shoreline trails and other attractions, such as Smith Falls, Nebraska's tallest waterfall. Soak in the atmosphere by standing underneath and letting the cold water blast you. You can also enjoy the river by canoeing or tubing.

(402) 376-1901, nps.gov/niob/index.htm

28

TRAVEL THE ROAD

TO THE COLLEGE WORLD SERIES

Teams in college baseball's top division mark the middle two weeks of June on their calendar with dreams of winning the national title at Omaha's TD Ameritrade Park. Omaha has been home to the College World Series since 1950. Growing from a few thousand fans watching the eight-team tournament, today national television covers every game and long lines of fans wait patiently to get into the general admission outfield bleachers. TD Ameritrade Park Omaha seats about twenty-three thousand fans, but almost every game is packed as fans cheer on their favorite college teams. To keep the CWS for another twenty-five years, city leaders decided to move the tournament from venerable Rosenblatt Stadium to downtown's TD Ameritrade beginning in 2011. Rosenblatt's memory lives on with a small baseball field at the former site of its home plate.

1200 Mike Fahey St., Omaha, NE 68102
(402) 554-4404, cwsomaha.com

FUN FACT

Local teams Creighton and Nebraska sometimes play in the College World Series, turning the usually neutral fans into homers rooting for the local schools. Creighton tied for third nationally in the 1991 CWS, while Nebraska has made three appearances in the tournament.

29

REPORT FOR FUN
AT FORT ROBINSON STATE PARK

From its days as an outpost during the American Indian Wars to becoming one of the most popular state parks in Nebraska, Fort Robinson State Park offers a slew of outdoor attractions. It has about twenty-two thousand acres of scenery, so you can go horseback riding, enjoy a wagon ride around the park, or take a hike among the bluffs and woods that overlook the former military fort. Visitors can also fish, swim, or boat at the park. Overnight, stay in a cabin or a room in the refurbished soldiers' quarters.

Fort Robinson's history spans more than seventy years. Opened in 1873 as a camp, its role changed in the mid-1880s when it became home to a regiment of Buffalo soldiers (African American troops). During World War I, the fort served as a training site for mules and donkeys. In World War II, it served as a prisoner-of-war camp for captured German soldiers. The fort closed in the late 1940s and became a state park in 1956.

3200 Hwy. 20, Crawford, NE 69339
(308) 665-2900, outdoornebraska.gov/fortrobinson

HISTORICAL NOTE

Lakota Sioux chief Crazy Horse was killed by an American soldier while imprisoned at Fort Robinson in 1877. The military said he died trying to escape, but Native Americans believe he was murdered.

30

EXPLORE THE WORLD
AT HENRY DOORLY ZOO & AQUARIUM

Watching elephants lumber over open space, working, playing, and providing a glimpse into their life in the wild, ranks as a major draw for visitors to Omaha's Henry Doorly Zoo & Aquarium. The pachyderms may be a popular attraction in the zoo's African Grasslands exhibit, but they are just a small part of what makes the zoo so popular. Giraffes roaming about, lions sunning themselves on rocks, and more await visitors to the exhibit that takes up about a third of the zoo's 160 acres. One of the world's largest and most popular zoos, Henry Doorly Zoo & Aquarium constantly strives to improve its twenty attractions for its seventeen thousand animals. Recent additions such as Asian Highlands, Children's Adventure Trails, and Meadowlark Theater join fan favorites such as Desert Dome, Lied Jungle Rainforest, and Gorilla Valley in keeping Omaha among the world's top five zoos.

3701 S. Tenth St., Omaha, NE 68107
(402) 733-8401, omahazoo.com

FUN FACT

Henry Doorly Zoo has long been involved with the biodiversity on the island of Madagascar. It is the only home to lemurs, who continue to be threatened by deforestation. In an attempt to help provide a safe area for the lemurs, the Omaha zoo has planted more than two million trees on the island, but the work never ends.

SOAK UP FUN
AT LAKE MCCONAUGHY

With about one hundred miles of shoreline and white, sandy beaches, Lake McConaughy is a water enthusiast's dream spot. Built in the late 1930s to hold water for a regional power company, Lake McConaughy State Recreation Area soon developed into a summer destination for Nebraskans and those from neighboring states. About twenty miles long and four miles wide, Lake McConaughy is perfect for fishing, swimming, boating, camping, and beach fun. You can spend time relaxing on the white-sand beaches, building sandcastles, sunning, or splashing around in the lake. You're likely to see all kinds of boats—from sailboats and pontoons to speed boats—on the water, which can reach a depth of about 140 feet at full capacity. You may also see parasailers and windsurfers. Outdoor enthusiasts enjoy catching fish such as rainbow trout, walleye, and catfish. During the fall and winter, hunting, ice skating, and backpacking take over.

1475 Hwy. 61 N., Ogallala, NE 69153
(308) 284-8800, outdoornebraska.gov/lakemcconaughy

FUN FACT

Known as the Little Lake and commonly overshadowed by Big Mac, Lake Ogallala offers water fun in its own right. With about five miles of shoreline, Lake Ogallala is about 1.5 miles long and a quarter-mile wide. With good fishing available, anglers look for rainbow trout and perch.

32

STOP AND SMELL THE FLOWERS
AT LAURITZEN GARDENS

If someone tells you that you need to stop and smell the flowers, Omaha's Lauritzen Gardens offers the perfect spot. With twenty gardens located across one hundred acres, the botanical garden is home to beautiful flowers, including a rose garden, peonies, and spring flowers. Open for nearly forty years, Lauritzen Gardens has Japanese, British, and Lithuanian gardens to showcase Omaha's international relationships. You can enjoy a walk through the gardens or buy a seat on a tram that leads you on a narrated tour of the grounds. Lauritzen Gardens refuses to rest on its laurels, seeking ways to improve visitors' experiences. Path of the Sun, a section of the arboretum, features tree carvings depicting Lithuanian folk story characters. A few years ago, Lauritzen Gardens added a glass-enclosed conservatory, which features plants and trees from temperate and tropical environments.

100 Bancroft St., Omaha, NE 68108
(402) 346-4002, lauritzengardens.org

FUN FACT

Each Christmas, Lauritzen Gardens showcases many types of poinsettias with a show that runs from Thanksgiving weekend until New Year's. The exhibit features a twenty-five-foot Christmas tree made of poinsettias.

VIEW BEAUTIFUL FLOWERS AND PLANTS
AT SUNKEN GARDENS

Originally a neighborhood landfill, Lincoln's Sunken Gardens ranks as one of the top botanical gardens in North America, according to *National Geographic*. During the Great Depression, a trio of Lincoln socialites donated the land to the city so it could become a rock garden. Local men cleared the land and later installed a rock garden. Developed in 1930, the terraced garden earned its name by being built in a natural depression. The garden eventually included flowers, as well. Today, with about thirty thousand flowers, plants, and trees, Sunken Gardens scores as the most beautiful 1.5 acres of land in any city. Using a new theme annually, the gardens include a rose garden, as well as water fountains and a pool featuring koi fish. The pavilion's dome depicts Lincoln's skyline.

South Twenty-Seventh Street and Capitol Parkway, Lincoln, NE 68502
(402) 441-8258, lincoln.ne.gov/city/parks/parksfacilities/publicgardens/sunken

34

GO BIG RED!

ROOT FOR THE HUSKERS

Game Day on a fall Saturday in Nebraska is almost as sacred as attending church on Sunday. Instead of wearing their Sunday best, thousands of loyal fans don their best red t-shirts, sweatshirts, and jackets as they root on one of the most successful football teams in college history. Nearly ninety thousand fans turn Memorial Stadium in Lincoln into the third-largest city in Nebraska as the Cornhuskers preach to their followers with a hard-fought game on Tom Osborne Field. Nebraska's football program ranks in the top ten all-time with nearly nine hundred wins. The team—with five national championships—also owns the college mark for consecutive sold-out games, with an ongoing record of more than 370 dating back to 1962.

Not to be outdone by football, Nebraska's volleyball team is a power in its own right. With five national championships, the Husker volleyball squad consistently ranks as one of the top programs in college sports, never having had a losing record since starting the sport in 1975. Since polls for college volleyball started in 1982, the Huskers have always been rated in the top twenty. Between the program's only three coaches, Nebraska has won more than thirteen hundred matches while losing less than 250.

One Memorial Stadium, 800 Stadium Dr., Lincoln, NE 68588
(402) 472-4224, huskers.com

DID YOU KNOW?

The University of Nebraska has won multiple national championships in several sports: women's bowling—twelve; men's gymnastics—eight; and women's track and field—two. The men's basketball team won the National Invitational Tournament championship in 1996.

Nebraska Division One College Programs

Creighton University

The Bluejays participate in the Big East. The men's basketball team annually challenges for NCAA tournament berths. The women's volleyball team is a top twenty-five program. Most sports compete for conference titles.
2500 California Plaza, Omaha, NE 68178
(402) 280-2700, gocreighton.com

University of Nebraska-Omaha

UNO—Omaha to its fans—competes in the Summit League for most sports. The Mavericks' hockey team participates in the National Collegiate Hockey Conference, where it has played in the Frozen Four (hockey's final four).
6001 Dodge St., Omaha, NE 68182
(402) 554-2001, omavs.com

TALK TO THE ANIMALS
AT THE LINCOLN CHILDREN'S ZOO

The Lincoln Children's Zoo has more than doubled its size with its expansion over the past couple of years. Expanding from just under nine acres to nineteen, the zoo has also increased its animal population, adding giraffes, tigers, spider monkeys, cheetahs, and anteaters to its impressive line-up. While visitors can't feed the giraffes, they can still get up close to animals that were here long before the African animals moved in. With lemurs, giant tortoises, alligators, and crocodiles calling the zoo home, visitors have long had an opportunity to see unique exhibits. The zoo's penguin exhibit is a must-see as the Humboldt penguins swim in an outdoor pool. You can also watch the animals down a ton of fish daily. While the zoo expanded, it kept its goal of providing a family-friendly experience with children's play areas.

1222 S. Twenty-Seventh St., Lincoln, NE 68502
(402) 475-6741, lincolnzoo.org

Lincoln Attractions

Lincoln Children's Museum
The Lincoln Children's Museum offers children an opportunity to play and learn with interactive exhibits.
1420 P St., Lincoln, NE 68508
(402) 477-4000, lincolnchildrensmuseum.org

Pioneers Park Nature Center
Home to an amphitheater, walking trails, wildlife viewing, and a visitor center, Pioneers Park offers something for everyone.
3201 S. Coddington Ave., Lincoln, NE 68522
(402) 441-7847, lincoln.ne.gov/city/parks/naturecenter/index.htm

Rock Island Train Wreck Site
On the Jamaica North Trail, a converted rail line that's part of the Lincoln trail system, a state historical marker recognizes the site of the deliberate and deadly derailment of a Rock Island train in 1894. The train had thirty-three passengers en route to Lincoln.
lincoln.ne.gov/city/parks/index.htm

National Museum of Roller Skating
Home to the world's largest collection of roller skates and memorabilia.
4730 South St., Lincoln, NE 68506
(402) 483-7551, rollerskatingmuseum.org

American Historical Society of Germans from Russia
Once a third of Lincoln's population, these European immigrants settled here because the climate reminded them of home. The museum shares the immigrants' culture and history.
631 D St., Lincoln, NE 68502
(402) 474-3363, ahsgr.org

EXPLORE NEBRASKA'S TOP PARK

AT MAHONEY STATE PARK

Attracting a million visitors annually, Eugene T. Mahoney State Park near Ashland strives to maintain its status as the "jewel" of the Nebraska state park system. While it's home to camping, cabins, trails, and fishing, Mahoney State Park has added several attractions in recent years to keep it relevant well into the twenty-first century. With a six-section zipline course, including an obstacle course with rope bridges, the park took a major step in attracting new visitors. A rock-climbing wall and a new aquatic center with three water slides give families an additional reason to visit the park. Traditional park visitors needn't worry, though. Mahoney State Park still offers horseback trail riding, as well as paddle boats at the marina. Summer visitors can also take in a show at the amphitheater. And, of course, the seventy-foot-tall observation tower continues to provide a majestic view of the Platte River valley.

28500 W. Park Hwy., Ashland, NE 68003
(402) 944-2523, outdoornebraska.gov/mahoney

Platte River State Park
14421 346th St.
Louisville, NE 68037
(402) 234-2217
outdoornebraska.gov/platteriver

Schramm Park State Recreation Area
21502 W. Hwy. 31
Gretna, NE 68028
(402) 332-5022
outdoornebraska.gov/schramm

Two Rivers State Recreation Area
27702 F St.
Waterloo, NE 68069
(402) 359-5165
outdoornebraska.gov/tworivers

Indian Cave State Park
65296 720 Rd.
Shubert, NE 68437
(402) 883-2575
outdoornebraska.gov/indiancave

Summit Lake State Recreation Area
2787 County Rd. G
Tekamah, NE 68061
(402) 374-1727
outdoornebraska.gov/summitlake

Ponca State Park
88090 Spur 26 E.
Ponca, NE 68770
(402) 755-2284
outdoornebraska.gov/ponca

Niobrara State Park
89261 522 Ave.
Niobrara, NE 68760
(402) 857-3373
outdoornebraska.gov/niobrara

Fort Kearny State Historical Park
1020 V Rd.
Kearney, NE 68847
(308) 865-5305
outdoornebraska.gov/fortkearny

Chadron State Park
15951 Hwy. 385
Chadron, NE 69337
(308) 432-6167
outdoornebraska.gov/chadron

Bowring Ranch State Historical Park
Highway 61
Merriman, NE 69218
(308) 684-3428
outdoornebraska.gov/bowringranch

37

TAKE IN BASEBALL
AT NEBRASKA'S FIELDS OF DREAMS

The road to major league dreams runs through Nebraska. From Triple-A baseball with its budding major league stars to a lower-level independent team, baseball fans relish taking in America's pastime. The Omaha Storm Chasers have called Papillion's Werner Park home since moving from Omaha's Rosenblatt Stadium in 2011. The team, known as the Royals for much of its five-decade operation, has been the Triple-A affiliate of the Kansas City Royals since starting play in 1969. The Storm Chasers have won Triple-A baseball's national championship twice in the past decade.

Down the road in Lincoln, the Saltdogs compete in the Single-A American Association. With young, upstart players seeking a chance to advance and gritty veterans hanging on for another opportunity, this team plays in a true "bus league," taking on teams in places such as Sioux City, Fargo, and Gary, Indiana. The Saltdogs truly play for the love of the game.

Omaha Storm Chasers
12356 Ballpark Way, Papillion, NE 68046
(402) 738-5100, milb.com/omaha

Lincoln Saltdogs
403 Line Dr., Lincoln, NE 68508
(402) 474-2255, saltdogs.com

Nebraska Sports Teams

Omaha Beef (indoor football)
7300 Q St., Ralston, NE 68127
(402) 346-2333, beeffootball.com

Omaha Lancers (hockey)
7300 Q St., Ralston, NE 68127
(402) 344-7825, lancers.com

Tri-City Storm (hockey)
609 Platte Rd., Kearney, NE 68845
(308) 338-8144, stormhockey.com

Lincoln Stars (hockey)
1880 Transformation Dr., Lincoln, NE 68508
(402) 474-7827, lincolnstars.com

Union Omaha (USL soccer)
12356 Ballpark Way, Papillion, NE 68046
(402) 884-8040, uniomahasc.com

38

CATCH THE CHECKERED FLAG

AT THE MUSEUM OF AMERICAN SPEED

From vintage motorcycles to classic Indy racers, the Speedway Motors Museum of American Speed rivals any major car collection. The museum's displays are the result of Bill Smith's sixty-year love affair with collecting cars and anything related to them. The museum, which opened in 1992, features several exhibits, such as hot rods, vintage dirt bikes, and rocket cars used to challenge speed records in the desert. Cars are displayed using themes, such as vehicles in an Indianapolis 500 pit area and a mechanic's garage. Besides race cars, the Museum of American Speed collection includes classic cars, such as the Tucker. It was considered the complete package, with features such as independent suspension and safety glass, but Tucker produced only fifty-one models. Another unique attraction is actress Hedy Lamarr's 1958 Cadillac. The museum also has a floor dedicated to toys such as classic pedal cars. Among the exhibits are old-school lunch boxes and autographed guitars.

599 Oakcreek Dr., Lincoln, NE 68528
(402) 323-3166, museumofamericanspeed.com

Midway between Lincoln and Omaha, I-80 Speedway showcases the area's best car racing each Friday night April through October. Fans pack in to watch exciting races on a dirt track and have a good time. I-80 Speedway, a NASCAR Home Track, features late models, stock cars, and hobby cars.

TAKE A COLD SHOWER
AT SMITH FALLS

Located about eighteen miles east of Valentine, sixty-three-foot-high Smith Falls stands as the tallest waterfall in Nebraska. Visitors access Smith Falls State Park via a historic footbridge across the Niobrara River. State officials relocated the former vehicle bridge from Verdigre and renovated it as a pedestrian bridge. The falls are popular with people floating along the river in kayaks, canoes, and inner tubes. People like to stand underneath as the cold water falls, giving them an icy shower that some may not be expecting. Smith Falls is located on the shady side of the river, thus cooling the spring-fed water. Smith Falls became a state park in 1992. The park, which was near the southern end of glacial ice, houses unique plants and trees more associated with climates farther north, such as paper birch and aspen. The state park is also popular with campers.

90165 Smith Falls Rd., Valentine, NE 69201
(402) 376-1306, outdoornebraska.gov/smithfalls

DID YOU KNOW?

Nebraska has more than 230 waterfalls across the state.

40

CHECK THE LINEUP OF STARS

AT THE MUSEUM OF NEBRASKA MAJOR LEAGUE BASEBALL

Cooperstown, New York, may be home to the professional baseball hall of fame, but the community of St. Paul honors Nebraska baseball legends with its own museum. Opened in 1999, the Museum of Nebraska Major League Baseball recognizes Nebraskans, including Bob Gibson and former St. Paul resident Grover Cleveland Alexander, who are members of the national hall of fame. Each of the honorees' exhibits includes personal and sports memorabilia. The museum also honors other Nebraskans who have played Major League Baseball, such as Alex Gordon, Joba Chamberlain, and Gregg Olson. More than one hundred Nebraskans are recognized at the museum.

619 Howard Ave., St. Paul, NE 68873
(308) 754-5558, nebraskabaseballmuseum.com

DID YOU KNOW?

Grover Cleveland Alexander spent twenty seasons in Major League Baseball and is still tied for the most wins in the National League with 373. Ronald Reagan and Doris Day starred in a movie based on Alexander, *The Winning Team*. St. Paul honors the local sports hero with a three-day festival each summer.

41

FLOAT ALONG NEBRASKA RIVERS
IN A COW TANK

If someone asks you if you want to take a float, they're not a Nebraskan. We call it tanking. No, you won't drive a military tank into the river; you'll hop inside a cow tank and float downriver. Cow tank? You betcha. Someone somewhere thought, "Hey, what if we took an empty cow watering tank, loaded it with a couple of chairs and put it in the river? Think it would float?" They did. And it does.

The round metal tank, normally used as a watering source for livestock on farms and ranches, has excellent buoyancy and floats along the water quite slowly, allowing you to take in the sights and enjoy time with friends and family. Shallow rivers are best suited for tanking, with rivers such as the Middle Loup, North Platte, Niobrara, and Elkhorn among the popular choices. Outfitters equip tanks with tables and chairs, so bring a cooler with drinks and snacks.

Calamus Outfitters (Calamus River)
83720 Valleyview Ave., Burwell, NE 68823
(308) 346-4697, calamusoutfitters.com

Crazy Rayz Tanking (Cedar River in the Sandhills)
82228 499 Ave., Spalding, NE 68665
(308) 571-0990, crazyrayztanks.com

Dusty Trails (North Platte River)
2617 N. Buffalo Bill Ave., North Platte, NE 69101
(308) 530-0048, dustytrails.biz

Get Tanked (Cedar River)
82379 Ericson-Scotia Ave., Ericson, NE 68637
(308) 750-5974, get-tanked.com

Sandhills Motel and Glidden Canoe Rental (Middle Loup River)
507 SW First St., Mullen, NE 69152
(308) 546-2206, sandhillsmotel.com

Tank Down the Elkhorn (Elkhorn River)
Omaha, NE 68145
(402) 709-8693, tankdown.com

378

CULTURE AND HISTORY

EXPLORE OMAHA'S HISTORY
AT THE DURHAM MUSEUM

At its height of travel shortly after World War II, about ten thousand people traveled through Omaha's Union Station. A decade later, train travel had all but dried up as more people traveled by automobile and then by airplane. By 1971, trains no longer stopped at Union Station. In 1973, Union Pacific Railroad donated the building to the city of Omaha, which renamed it The Durham Museum. The art deco building soon served a new purpose—showcasing Omaha's history. Today, The Durham pays homage to its railroad days with a replica of Union Station's depot. In the lower level, exhibits cover a variety of topics, including the 1898 Trans-Mississippi and International Exposition (World's Fair).

801 S. Tenth St., Omaha, NE 68108
(402) 444-5071, durhammuseum.org

DID YOU KNOW?

Omaha's rail history dates back to the early 1860s, when it was selected as the eastern terminus of what became the Union Pacific Railroad. Local leaders lobbied hard to get the railroad over Omaha's Iowa neighbor, Council Bluffs, where Union Pacific now operates its history museum.

Omaha Attractions

Joslyn Castle

Lyndhurst, as its owners called the mansion, was built to resemble a Scottish castle. It was nicknamed Joslyn Castle by locals after George and Sarah Joslyn, the owners.
3902 Davenport St., Omaha, NE 68131
(402) 595-2199, joslyncastle.com

El Museo Latino

This museum shares the history and culture of Omaha's Latino community.
4701 S. Twenty-Fifth St., Omaha, NE 68107
(402) 731-1137, elmuseolatino.org

Boys Town Hall of History

This museum shares Boys Town's history, from Father Flanagan's home for boys in central Omaha to its current campus, which houses both boys and girls.
14057 Flanagan Blvd., Boys Town, NE 68010
(402) 498-1300, boystown.org

Omaha Children's Museum

A space for children to play while they learn about science, math, and other topics, the Omaha Children's Museum also offers special exhibits on topics such as interactive sports and dinosaurs.
500 S. Twentieth St., Omaha, NE 68102
(402) 342-6164, ocm.org

Sarpy County Museum

This museum chronicles the history of Nebraska's third-largest county.
2402 Clay St., Bellevue, NE 68005
(402) 292-1880, sarpycountymuseum.org

43

HAVE FUN WITH SCIENCE
AT EDGERTON EXPLORIT CENTER

Have you seen the famous photograph of a bullet speeding through an apple? Or a splash of milk creating a crown shape? If so, you can thank Aurora's Harold "Doc" Edgerton. As a scientist, Edgerton invented the strobe light and stroboscope, which advanced the art of stop-motion and high-speed photography. As a graduate of the Massachusetts Institute of Technology, Edgerton worked on a number of inventions during his career, including deep-sea photography. In honor of his work, National Geographic named Edgerton one of the top fifteen inventors of the twentieth century.

Opened in 1995, the Edgerton Explorit Center serves as a hands-on science center in honor of Edgerton. It offers more than thirty interactive science exhibits that appeal to people of all ages. The Explorit Center makes learning science easy and fun because you don't realize how much information you're absorbing while playing a game or examining one of their interactive exhibits, such as static electricity.

208 Sixteenth St., Aurora, NE 68818
(402) 694-4032, edgerton.org

You can learn about the history of Central Nebraska pioneers at the Plainsman Museum in Aurora. With exhibits featuring early settlers from the 1800s through the mid-1900s, the museum explores farm life as well as small-town businesses.

LEARN ABOUT NATIVE AMERICAN HISTORY AT GENOA INDIAN SCHOOL

Open for fifty years, the Genoa Indian School represents a sad chapter in American history when the federal government forced Native American children to leave their homes and attend boarding schools that taught the English language and European-American culture. While most boarding schools were on reservations, the Genoa school was one of four non-reservation schools. Tasked with educating fewer than one hundred students when it opened in 1889, by the time it closed in 1934 Genoa had nearly six hundred enrolled students from more than twenty tribes in nearly a dozen states. Today the Genoa Indian School Interpretive Center offers an accurate look at life at the school, including a replica of a classroom, as well as artifacts.

209 Webster Ave., Genoa, NE 68640
(402) 993-6036, facebook.com/Genoa-US-Indian-School-Foundation-218630092006

DID YOU KNOW?

Nebraska is home to four federally recognized tribes—the Ponca, Omaha, Winnebago, and Santee Sioux.

TRAVEL BACK IN TIME

AT AGATE FOSSIL BEDS NATIONAL MONUMENT

Long before Native Americans and pioneers traveled across the Nebraska plains, prehistoric animals roamed a Serengeti-like region in the panhandle. Dating back nearly twenty million years, animals that resembled pig-bison and bear-dog, as well as miniature rhinoceroses, lived near a large watering hole there. But the source dried up, killing nearby vegetation. And with their food and water sources gone, the animals eventually succumbed. Today, Agate Fossil Beds National Monument marks the site of a major fossil discovery with walking trails to the primary dig sites at Carnegie Hill and University Hill, and to the site of dryland beavers' burrows.

301 River Rd., Harrison, NE 69346
(308) 665-4113, nps.gov/agfo/index.htm

NATIVE AMERICAN COLLECTION

Located at the tributary that becomes the Niobrara River, Agate Fossils Bed National Monument is home to a five-hundred-piece Native American collection that once belonged to James H. Cook. The local rancher, who once owned the land that is now the park, befriended—and received gifts from—Native Americans such as Lakota chief Red Cloud.

46

REVISIT THE DEUCE
ON OMAHA'S TWENTY-FOURTH STREET

Omaha's Twenty-Fourth and Lake Street area bustled with businesses in the early 1900s. Impacted by an Easter Sunday tornado in 1913, the Near North Side rebuilt and continued its winning ways. Although it was primarily an African American community, people of all ethnic groups got along well and ran businesses side by side. Home to Omaha's best music halls, such as the Carnation, Dreamland, and Showcase ballrooms, it hosted major performers such as Count Basie, Duke Ellington, Ella Fitzgerald, and Nat King Cole. Then, in a series of events, such as economic downturns and civil rights struggles, many businesses closed or moved. Recently, however, the Near North Side has seen an economic upturn, with new businesses opening in and relocating to the neighborhood, including the Great Plains Black History Museum. Now, the music scene is alive and well at Love's Jazz and Art Center. Restoration Exchange tours offer a look into the area's history, highlighting more than thirty buildings listed on the National Register of Historic Places.

DID YOU KNOW?

Civil rights leader Malcolm X was born in Omaha. Born Malcolm Little, his family moved away from Omaha early in his childhood after his father, a minister, was harassed and threatened by the Ku Klux Klan. He turned to Islam as an adult and later took the name Malcolm X. He was thirty-nine years old when he was assassinated in 1965.

Restoration Exchange
3902 Davenport St., Omaha, NE 68131
(402) 933-3104, restorationexchange.org/events/walking-tours

Great Plains Black History Museum
2505 N. Twenty-Fourth St., Omaha, NE 68110
(402) 932-7077, gpblackhistorymuseum.org

Love's Jazz and Art Center
2510 N. Twenty-Fourth St., Omaha, NE 68111
(402) 502-5291, ljac.org

47

EXPLORE AGRICULTURE'S APPEAL TO ART

AT THE BONE CREEK MUSEUM OF AGRARIAN ART

As the country's only museum connecting people to the land through art, the Bone Creek Museum of Agrarian Art celebrates the work of artist Dale Nichols. The David City native focused his art, including paintings, lithographs, and wood carvings, on farm life. Enthusiasts of regionalism consider his landscape paintings to be as important as works by other notable Midwestern artists, such as Grant Wood, who's best known for *American Gothic*. The Bone Creek Museum opened in 2007, a dozen years after Nichols passed away at the age of ninety-one. As the national center for Nichols's collection, the museum also features the work of other artists who highlight rural life, as well as magazine covers for *Fortune* magazine published between 1930 and 1950. The museum also sponsors special exhibitions that showcase contemporary regional artists.

575 E St., David City, NE 68632
(402) 367-4488, bonecreek.org

EXPLORE PLAINS LIFE
AT THE MARI SANDOZ HIGH PLAINS HERITAGE CENTER

The author of more than twenty books about life on the plains, from a biography of her father to stories about Native American and pioneer life, Mari Sandoz realistically described life in the Midwest. Considered one of the best writers of her time, Sandoz injected life into her stories. The Mari Sandoz High Plains Heritage Center in Chadron honors the Nebraska native. The former Carnegie library offers insight into Sandoz's work and life through a series of exhibits. The heritage center also provides a look into her father's paleontology research and her sister's love of botany, as she would explore and examine the wildflowers around the Sandhills ranch. Outside, the center features a Heritage Garden with native plants, as well as immigrant plants introduced to the plains by settlers. Located at Chadron State College, the center also hosts conferences.

Chadron State College
1000 Main St., Chadron, NE 69337
(308) 432-6401, sandozcenter.com

VISIT BROWNVILLE:
THE TOWN ON THE NATIONAL REGISTER OF HISTORIC PLACES

How does an entire town get listed on the National Register of Historic Places? Established in the mid-1800s, Brownville became a major port along the Missouri River. Business boomed, and the town grew to almost two thousand people. Then a new port opened upriver in Nebraska City. The anticipated railroad never came. And, to top it off, the local ferry boat sank. Not surprisingly, the population dwindled. Today, with a population of about 150 people, Brownville has reinvented itself. Named to the National Register in 1970 because of the historical significance of several buildings, today Brownville attracts tourists with the art galleries, bookstores, boutiques, and restaurants occupying those same buildings. Whiskey Run Creek Winery and Distillery operates in a barn that dates back more than a hundred years. You can also explore the area's trails or walk through an arboretum established in the 1990s.

(402) 825-1240, brownville-ne.com

FUN FACT

Brownville celebrates the holidays with festive decorations around town, capped with a Christmas Gala concert featuring national performers.

50

VISIT
PRESIDENT GERALD FORD'S BIRTHSITE AND GARDENS

While Gerald Ford's family moved away from Omaha a few weeks after his birth, Omaha embraced him as one of its own. The only person to act as vice president and then president of the United States without being elected, Ford also served for twenty-five years in Congress. Named to succeed Spiro Agnew as vice president following Agnew's resignation in late 1973, Ford ascended to the presidency about nine months later when Richard M. Nixon resigned because of the Watergate scandal. Serving as the thirty-eighth president, Ford lost the 1976 election to Jimmy Carter. Ford's childhood home succumbed to fire in 1971. To honor the former president, organizers created the Gerald R. Ford Birthsite and Gardens, which includes information about Ford's life, as well as a rose garden in memory of former first lady Betty Ford.

3202 Woolworth Ave., Omaha, NE 68105
(402) 444-5955, history.nebraska.gov/blog/gerald-r-ford-conservation-center-and-birthsite

DID YOU KNOW?

Nebraska has had its share of presidential candidates. William Jennings Bryan was a three-time nominee for the Democratic Party, losing each time. Bob Kerrey, a former governor, sought the 1992 Democratic nomination before bowing out during the primary season.

FRED'S FLYING CIRCUS (page 143)

GRAIN BIN ANTIQUE TOWN (page 125)

OMAHA STORM CHASERS (page 58)

CHIEF STANDING BEAR (page 134)

BAKERS CANDIES (page 4)

LINCOLN HIGHWAY (page 106)
BEFORE
LINCOLN
L
HIGHWAY

JOHNNY CARSON EXHIBIT (page 112)

HIGGINS MEMORIAL (page 105)

KOOL-AID EXHIBIT (page 116)

STUHR MUSEUM LIVING HISTORY TOWN (page 142)

STARKE ROUND BARN (page 139)

BUFFALO BILL RANCH STATE HISTORICAL PARK (page 124)

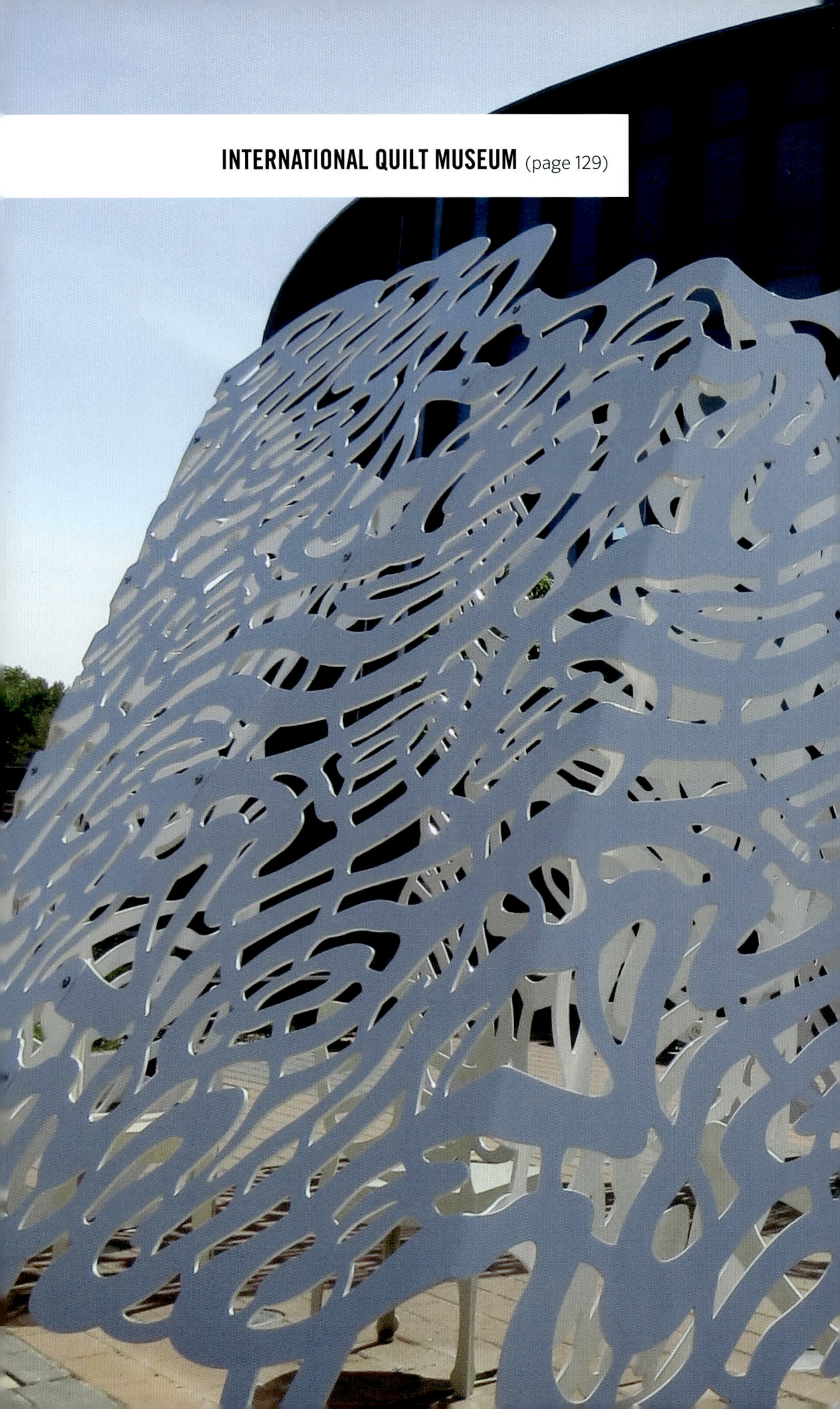
INTERNATIONAL QUILT MUSEUM (page 129)

NEBRASKA FOOTBALL (page 52)

GENOA INDIAN SCHOOL (page 72)

51

CELEBRATE CINCO DE MAYO IN SOUTH OMAHA

The first weekend in May, thousands of people line South Twenty-Fourth Street in South Omaha to watch a Cinco de Mayo parade that lasts up to two hours—one of the largest parades in the Midwest. The parade includes floats, mariachi bands, people performing traditional dances, and vaqueros on horseback, as well as civic groups and politicians tossing candy to children. More than seventy-five thousand people attend the three-day Cinco de Mayo festival to celebrate Mexican heritage and culture. Featuring carnival rides, music, dances, and food, the celebration is truly an event where all Latin American cultures are embraced. South Omaha has a history of welcoming immigrants from Eastern Europe, Germany, Ireland, and Italy, and it is a true melting pot. The neighborhood also shares its history through a series of murals.

South Omaha Museum, 2314 M St., Omaha, NE 68107
(402) 734-3240, cincodemayoomaha.com

FUN FACT

Omaha's Hispanic community has hosted festivals and celebrations since the 1920s.

Nebraska's Ethnic Festivals

Sōl Food and Music Festival

Hosted each summer at the birthplace of civil rights leader Malcolm X, the event celebrates the African American community through food and music.

Malcolm X Foundation

3448 Evans St., Omaha, NE 68111

(800) 645-9287, malcolmxfoundation.org

Native Omaha Days Festival

Held every two years, the Native Omaha Days Festival celebrates the neighborhoods of North Omaha. With a parade, music, dances, and food, the celebration welcomes all residents and former residents of North Omaha in a homecoming reunion.

Native Omahans Club, Inc.

3819 ½ N. Twenty-Fourth St., Omaha, NE 68110

(402) 457-5974, nativeomahadays.org

Nebraska Asian Festival

Highlighting the Asian influence in Omaha, this annual event is hosted along the Omaha Riverfront.

Lewis and Clark Landing

345 Riverfront Dr., Omaha, NE 68102

(402) 216-9081, nebraskaasianfestival.com

Omaha's Original Greek Festival

Celebrating Omaha's Greek community through music, dance, and food, this annual event is hosted at St. John the Baptist Greek Orthodox Church.

602 Park Ave., Omaha, NE 68105

(402) 345-710, greekfestomaha.com

52

LEARN ABOUT THE RISE AND FALL OF ROME

AT THE CLAYTON MUSEUM OF ANCIENT HISTORY

When donating his collection of historical artifacts that he believed proved the Bible to be historically accurate, C. Foster Stanback sought the perfect location and relationship to support his beliefs. Former York College wrestling coach Ramon Diaz recommended the school because he believed it met his friend's requirements. Open since 2015, the Clayton Museum of Ancient History has a collection of 230 pieces dating from 3000 BC to the early 1600s. Exhibits feature Roman soldiers' weapons, leaves from the Erasmus New Testament and King James Bible, coins, and statues. The collection offers a look into life during the rise and fall of the Roman Empire. The Clayton Museum of Ancient History also includes Little Kingdom, an interactive area where children can participate in an archaeological dig and a weekly story time.

York College's Phyllis Mackey Center, 1125 E. Eighth St., York, NE 68467
(402) 363-5748, claytonmuseumofancienthistory.org

York Attractions

Lee's Legendary Marbles

Lee's is home to the world's largest collection of marbles. You can also find other unique items among its eclectic collections.

3120 S. Lincoln Ave., York, NE 68467

(402) 362-3320, leeslegendarymarbles.com

Wessels Living History Farm

The Wessels Living History Farm shares a look at farming in the Midwest during the 1920s. Visitors can tour historical buildings on the farm and view farm equipment.

5520 S. Lincoln Ave., York, NE 68467

(402) 710-0682, livinghistoryfarm.org

York Water Tower

Painted to resemble a hot air balloon, the York water tower has taken on a life of its own and become a popular tourist stop. It is located just north of I-80, at the south end of Broadwell Avenue.

RELIVE LIFE AS A HOMESTEADER AT DOWSE SOD HOUSE

President Abraham Lincoln signed the Homestead Act into law in 1862, opening up the West for settlement. As pioneers sought new lives on the Midwestern plains, the lack of trees prevented them from building traditional houses. Instead, they used local resources, which in Nebraska's case meant sod. Most sod houses were basic structures, with four walls and a dirt floor. But others included more refined designs, including separate rooms. In 1900, William R. Dowse designed his home near Comstock to include the amenities you'd expect in a home today. With wood floors and a wood-burning stove, the Dowse sod house was occupied until the last family member left in 1959. After about two decades of neglect, the house was renovated to its former self. Today, visitors can enjoy a walk through pioneer history.

80560 Oak Grove Rd., Comstock, NE 68828
(308) 215-0365, facebook.com/pages/Dowse-Sod-House/393185474070538

COMSTOCK WINDMILL FESTIVAL

Located in a canyon near the small village of Comstock, Second Wind Ranch is home to dozens of vintage windmills. The land provides the setting for the annual Comstock Windmill Festival, a three-day outdoor country-music festival each summer. Attracting thousands of people from around the Midwest, the festival, which started more than twenty years ago, has attracted performers such as Brad Paisley.

54

CZECH OUT

WILBER'S CZECH DAYS

Widely considered the state's Czech capital, Wilber celebrates Czech history and culture over a four-day weekend each August. From a beer garden to parades held over two days, Czech Days encourages visitors to become Czech during their visit. You'll find people wearing traditional folk outfits around town as you explore food, folk dancing, music, and special exhibits. Visit Wilber's past at the Wilber Czech Museum, home to nearly two thousand artifacts and pieces of memorabilia, such as household items and traditional clothing. Murals painted on downtown buildings also help tell the small town's story. Now a bed and breakfast, the Hotel Wilber offers a look at the town's past with its European decor. Savoring the taste, people stand in line outside Frank's Smokehouse for an authentic handmade Czech sausage or kolache (jam-filled pastry).

Wilber Czech Museum, 101 W. Third St., Wilber, NE 68465
(402) 821-2732, nebraskaczechsofwilber.com

FUN FACT

Even with a population of around two thousand, Wilber has produced some notable residents, such as Dana Altman, who has coached NCAA basketball teams at Kansas State University, Creighton, and the University of Oregon. Another famous resident is C. L. Edson, who served as a newspaper columnist in New York in the early twentieth century. His autobiography was titled *The Great American Ass.*

Nebraska Celebrations

Polish Days

The Polish capital of Nebraska, Loup City, celebrates its Eastern European heritage over three days in June. Parades, food, music, and dances are the highlights of the event.
133 S. Eighth St., Loup City, NE 68853
(308) 745-0430, loupcitychamber.org

Oktoberfest

Omaha's German-American Society hosts this annual two-day event in September. Highlights include traditional music and food, as well as drinks.
3717 S. 120th St., Omaha, NE 68144
(402) 333-6615, germanamericansociety.org

La Festa Italiana

This Omaha festival celebrates locals' Italian heritage over Labor Day weekend with authentic food, music, games, and fireworks.
5110 N. 132nd St., Omaha, NE 68164
(402) 493-8888, omahaitaly.com

St. Patrick's Day Celebration in O'Neill

The Irish capital of Nebraska, O'Neill, celebrates St. Patrick's Day with a two-day event featuring a pipes-and-drum performance on a giant shamrock downtown, a parade, and recognition of the festival's royalty.

O'Neill Chamber of Commerce

125 S. Fourth St., O'Neill, NE 68763
(402) 336-2355, oneillchamber.com

55

WALK THROUGH HISTORY

IN MCCOOK'S HERITAGE SQUARE

Small-town Nebraska proudly celebrates its residents who serve the state in elected office. McCook thumps its chest with a little more pride than other communities because it was the home of George Norris, the inventor of the state's unique unicameral (one-house) legislature. Nebraskans approved Norris's idea in the mid-1930s. Norris served in the US Congress for forty years, spending five terms in the US House of Representatives and another five terms in the Senate. Following his political career, he returned to McCook. Another US senator also called McCook home: Ben Nelson grew up in town before becoming Nebraska's governor and then a two-term US senator. Their homes are the highlights of a self-guided tour of the ten-block Heritage Square. Also included on the tour, Frank Lloyd Wright's Sutton House and the Museum of the High Plains showcase unique architectural designs. You can pick up maps at the museum.

421 Norris Ave., McCook, NE 69001
(308) 345-3661, facebook.com/MuseumOfTheHighPlains

SALUTE A HERO
AT THE HIGGINS MEMORIAL

While Andrew Jackson Higgins never fired a shot, former president and five-star general Dwight D. Eisenhower credited him as the man who won World War II. Higgins, a Columbus native, invented the Higgins Boat, an amphibious landing craft that carried soldiers from naval ships to the beaches of Normandy during the D-Day invasion of France. Eisenhower believed that the Higgins Boat had played a major role in D-Day's success. The US military used the Higgins Boat through the Korean War.

Columbus honors its native son with a special memorial at Pawnee Park, featuring a life-size replica of the Higgins Boat with soldiers emerging from it. The Andrew Jackson Higgins Memorial also includes sand from the French beach. The memorial anchors the park, which also honors military veterans, as well as the victims and heroes of the September 11, 2001, terrorist attacks.

West Pawnee Park, Columbus, NE 68601
(402) 564-2769, higginsmemorial.com

FUN FACT

Columbus celebrated 150 years of history with a downtown mural that was unveiled during its sesquicentennial in 2006. The mural traces key moments in the city's development.

57

DRIVE AMERICA'S FIRST TRANSCONTINENTAL HIGHWAY

ON US 30

Stretching across Nebraska, US 30—the Lincoln Highway—was the first transcontinental highway in the United States. Construction began in 1913 and covered more than three thousand miles from New York City to San Francisco. Nebraska is home to about 450 of those miles. Originally running from Omaha to the Wyoming border, US 30 now runs from Blair to the western border. Unique attractions along the highway include a mile-long section of the original brick in Elkhorn. Farther west, Grand Island paved the second mile of the highway—a seedling mile—so US 30 would include the community. Cities continue to spark tourism along the highway with attractions such as Kearney's Classic Car Collection museum.

lincolnhighwaynebraskabyway.com

DID YOU KNOW?

Nebraska was one of thirteen states involved with the Lincoln Highway, also known as America's Main Street. It took several years for the transcontinental highway to be paved, but that didn't stop people from driving it.

58

FARM THE LAND
AT THE HOMESTEAD NATIONAL MONUMENT

Imagine having the opportunity to get 160 acres of land for free. The only catch is that you have just five years to develop the land and build a house. President Abraham Lincoln signed the Homestead Act into law in 1862. After convincing a clerk to open the land office shortly after midnight on New Year's Day, 1863, Daniel Freeman filed the nation's first homestead claim, for land near Beatrice. Recognizing the achievement, the Homestead National Monument opened on the very land Freeman farmed until his death in 1908. Visitors can explore historical buildings, including a one-room schoolhouse, and trails through fields of prairie grass. While Freeman succeeded, most people failed at homesteading, which occurred in thirty states through the mid-1980s.

8523 W. State Hwy. 4, Beatrice, NE 68310
(402) 223-3514, nps.gov/home

FUN FACT

Before he was a movie and television star, Robert Taylor called Beatrice home. Born in Filley as Spangler Arlington Brugh, Taylor and his family moved around before settling in Beatrice. After becoming a star high school athlete, Taylor eventually settled in Hollywood, where he starred in movies alongside legends such as Irene Dunne, Greta Garbo, Lana Turner, Richard Widmark, and James Whitmore. He also appeared in television series such as *The Detectives* and *Death Valley Days*.

59

LEARN ABOUT THE BIRTHPLACE OF ARBOR DAY

AT ARBOR LODGE

From creating Arbor Day to founding Morton Salt, J. Sterling Morton and his family left their mark on Nebraska and the nation. But everything began with a small cabin in Nebraska City that would eventually grow into a mansion. Arbor Lodge State Historical Park celebrates the life of Morton, who worked as a newspaper editor before founding Arbor Day. Morton also served as a Nebraska territorial governor and as the agriculture secretary during President Grover Cleveland's second administration in the 1890s.

Morton built the four-room cabin after settling in Nebraska City as a young man. His son Joy, the founder of Morton Salt, later built a mansion that encompassed the cabin. Among the fifty-two rooms was a one-lane bowling alley in the basement. Joy later donated the mansion—which resembled the White House—and its grounds to the state, with the stipulation that it be used to honor his father. Today, thousands visit Arbor Lodge and its arboretum each year.

2600 Arbor Ave., Nebraska City, NE 68410
(402) 873-7222, outdoornebraska.gov/arborlodge

FUN FACT

J. Sterling Morton's sons were successful in their own right. Joy founded Morton Salt, and his brother Mark partnered with him in several business ventures. A third son, Paul, served as secretary of the Navy during Teddy Roosevelt's presidency. And Carl, the fourth son, helped create the Argo Starch Company before passing away at the age of thirty-six.

Nebraska City Attractions

Kregel Windmill Factory Museum

This museum is the last known wooden windmill factory of its kind. The museum features the assembly area where employees built the windmills.

1416 Central Ave., Nebraska City, NE 68410

(402) 873-1078, kregelwindmillfactorymuseum.org

Mayhew Cabin with John Brown's Cave

This museum examines Nebraska City's role in the Underground Railroad, which helped escaped slaves find new homes in the North during the mid-1800s.

2012 Fourth Corso, Nebraska City, NE 68410

(402) 873-3115, mayhewcabin.org

Civil War Veterans Museum

This downtown museum offers a look at the Civil War.

910 First Corso, Nebraska City, NE 68410

(402) 873-4018, civilwarmuseumnc.org

Missouri River Basin Lewis and Clark Visitor Center

Relive the days when Lewis and Clark explored the Missouri River in the Nebraska City area.

100 Valmont Dr., Nebraska City, NE 68410

(402) 874-9900, lewisandclarkvisitorcenter.org

VISIT A POET LAUREATE'S STUDY

AT THE JOHN G. NEIHARDT STATE HISTORIC SITE

John G. Neihardt wrote more than two dozen books of poems and stories. Yet one work seems to define his career: *Black Elk Speaks* chronicles the oral history and traditions of the Lakota based on a series of interviews with Black Elk, a medicine man. *Black Elk Speaks* was only one of a five-volume set called *A Cycle of the West*, which explored life in the western United States. As a tribute to his work, Nebraska honored Neihardt as the state's poet laureate in 1921. A visit to the John G. Neihardt State Historic Site offers a look at the poet's life and career, including the one-room study where he worked. The visitor center houses *Hoop of the World*, an exhibit exploring Native American life.

306 W. Elm St., Bancroft, NE 68004
(402) 648-3388, neihardtcenter.org

DID YOU KNOW?

The nearby Omaha tribe reservation was the home of the first Native American woman to become a doctor. Susan La Flesche Picotte became a physician in 1889, when she was twenty-four. There are plans to honor her legacy by renovating a former hospital building in Walthill, where Dr. Picotte practiced during her career.

BECOME AN ART EXPERT
AT THE JOSLYN ART MUSEUM

A visit to Omaha's Joslyn Art Museum offers a look at both classical and modern art, from an original Rembrandt portrait to an outdoor sculpture garden. The European art collection dates back to the seventeenth century, and Omahans consider themselves fortunate to have a world-class art museum. Sarah Joslyn donated the museum to the city in honor of her husband, George. The museum, which has been open for nearly ninety years, actually started as a music hall with an art gallery but has since grown into a popular museum. While its collections range from ancient Egyptian art to Asian pieces, the Joslyn has outstanding pop and modern art, including a "dango" sculpture by local artist Jun Kaneko. With its permanent collection among the best of any American museum, the Joslyn Art Museum also hosts special exhibitions of art from around the world.

2200 Dodge St., Omaha, NE 68102
(402) 342-3300, joslyn.org

CONTEMPORARY ART SCENE

Omaha is home to several outstanding modern art galleries. The Kaneko in the Old Market is home to the works of Jun Kaneko, as well as hosting special exhibitions several times a year. The Bemis Center for Contemporary Arts, near the Kaneko, hosts contemporary exhibitions, as well as special in-house artists.

HEEEERE'S JOHNNY!

VISIT JOHNNY CARSON'S HOMETOWN

Johnny Carson hosted *The Tonight Show* on NBC for thirty years, but his entertainment career started in Nebraska. Born in Iowa, Carson and his family moved to Norfolk when he was eight years old, and he considered the northeast Nebraska community his hometown. Proud of his Nebraska heritage, Carson donated parts of his television stage, his Emmy awards, and other memorabilia to the Elkhorn Valley Museum in Norfolk, where they serve as a major exhibit. Norfolk hosts the annual Great American Comedy Festival—featuring famous comedians—each June at the Johnny Carson Theatre at the high school. His childhood home has been renovated and is recognized with a sign in the front yard.

Downtown, visitors can take in Carson's television career through a series of murals, beginning with a black-and-white one highlighting his start on an Omaha television station and concluding with his final *Tonight Show* episode.

515 Queen City Blvd., Norfolk, NE 68701
(402) 371-3886, elkhornvalleymuseum.org

DID YOU KNOW?

Norfolk isn't the hometown of just Johnny Carson. The area has been home to several famous people, including the Hall brothers, who founded Hallmark greeting cards, and Thurl Ravenscroft, who served as the voice of Tony the Tiger for Frosted Flakes cereal and sang "You're a Mean One, Mr. Grinch." The creator of Kewpie dolls, Rose O'Neill, also hailed from Norfolk. Her family moved there when she was three. And native son Orville Carlisle created the first model rocket.

CROSS THE PLAINS
AT THE ARCHWAY IN KEARNEY

Crossing I-80 as an example of pioneer determination to travel across the plains, The Archway explores westward migration through a series of exhibits, some interactive. You get a feel for what to expect as you ride the escalator to the main exhibit; mannequins dressed as pioneers seem to be climbing a steep hill to reach others in their wagon train. You'll see what families went through as they moved west to start new lives: women and children pushing covered wagons through mud and muck, for example, as a man tries to drive the oxen pulling the wagon. In the background, lightning flashes across an endless sea of prairie grass. The museum eventually jumps to a new migration period—the 1950s—when people started driving cross country on US 30. A drive-in theater and diner represent the conveniences of the twentieth century.

3060 E. First St., Kearney, NE 68847
(308) 237-1000, archway.org

FUN FACT

President Bill Clinton visited The Archway in December 2000, making Nebraska the final state he visited during his eight years as the chief executive of the United States.

Kearney Attractions

Classic Car Collection

The Classic Car Collection on US 30 houses more than two hundred vintage vehicles, including about a hundred cars and other types of vehicles on public display. The museum displays the cars—from early vehicles to recent models—in scenes such as a drive-in theater, gas station, and classic downtown.
3600 E. Hwy. 30, Ste. B, Kearney, NE 68847
(308) 234-1964, www.classiccarcollection.org

Museum of Nebraska Art

The MONA highlights the work of Nebraska natives or artists with a Nebraska connection. With special exhibitions the museum routinely offers something fresh. The impressive outdoor sculpture garden includes a statue of Clifton Hillegass, who founded CliffsNotes.
2401 Central Ave., Kearney, NE 68847
(308) 865-8559, mona.unk.edu

Fort Kearny State Historical Park

Playing a variety of roles, from an outfitting depot during the American Indian Wars to a Pony Express stop, Fort Kearny is remembered with a state park. Home to replicas of a stockade and blacksmith shop, Fort Kearny also has a parade area. It's a great spot for crane watching during the sandhill crane migration.
A state park permit is required to visit.
1020 V Rd., Kearney, NE 68847
(308) 865-5305, outdoornebraska.gov/fortkearny

G. W. Frank Museum of History and Culture

A businessman, George W. Frank, built this house for his parents. But George Sr. lost the house in the late 1800s following a nationwide economic collapse. Designed in Richardsonian Romanesque Shingle style, the house features Colorado red sandstone from Wyoming. Once a sanitorium, the house now is part of the University of Nebraska-Kearney and is open for tours.
2010 University Dr., Kearney, NE 68849
(308) 865-8441, unk.edu/offices/frankhouse

OPEN YOUR OWN KOOL-AID STAND

IN HASTINGS

Remember having a Kool-Aid stand when you were younger? Ever lick the dry powder in a Kool-Aid packet? If so, you need to visit Hastings. The Central Nebraska city where Edward Perkins invented the sweet drink mix loves to celebrate being the home of Kool-Aid. It hosts the annual Kool-Aid Days, a three-day event of all things Kool-Aid, including a parade, games, and concerts. You can even buy your favorite flavor at the world's largest Kool-Aid stand. Head to the Hastings Museum to explore the large exhibit that celebrates Perkins's invention, which he initially called Kool-Ade. With flavors such as cherry, grape, lemon, and root beer, the drink mix originally sold for ten cents a pack. The exhibit includes a replica of the general store Perkins's father operated in Hendley. The museum also displays Kool-Aid merchandise and costumes worn by the famous Kool-Aid Man.

Hastings Museum
1330 N. Burlington Ave.
Hastings, NE 68901, (402) 461-2399, hastingsmuseum.org

EXPLORE
LIKE LEWIS AND CLARK

Meriwether Lewis and William Clark led an expedition in the early 1800s to explore new territory along the Missouri River, and you can take your own journey along their path. The Lewis and Clark Scenic Byway runs for nearly ninety miles from Fort Calhoun to South Sioux City. As you explore historic locations such as Fort Atkinson in Fort Calhoun, where Lewis and Clark met with local Native American tribes, you can relive history through live reenactments. A stop in Blair offers a scenic nature walk at Black Elk-Neihardt Park. While traveling the byway, stop in Tekamah to track the expedition's progress on a building-sized mural. Farther north, visit the Omaha and Winnebago Indian reservations, which include a beautiful view of the Missouri River. To complete the journey, head north to South Sioux City, home to Freedom Park and its half-scale replica of the Vietnam Veterans Memorial.

Fort Atkinson State Historical Park
201 S. Seventh St., Fort Calhoun, NE 68023
(402) 468-5611, fortatkinsononline.org

FUN FACT

Fort Atkinson was the first American military fort established west of the Missouri River. The fort opened in 1827 and was operational for eight years.

SALUTE THE ARMY
AT THE HEARTLAND MUSEUM OF MILITARY VEHICLES

With more than one hundred military vehicles onsite, the Heartland Museum of Military Vehicles could easily be mistaken for the motor pool of a military base. But make no mistake: the museum is far from a maintenance shop. As you explore the Lexington museum, you'll experience history through vehicles, ranging from Jeeps to tanks and helicopters, that saw action in World War II and in Korea and Vietnam. While the majority of vehicles are American, some come from other nations, including two German vehicles used for desert warfare. The museum, which opened in 1986, expanded to a permanent location five years later. While the museum's main draw is the vehicles, it also offers exhibits on artifacts such as uniforms and helmets. The museum's popular M*A*S*H exhibit includes replicas of the television series' sets.

606 Heartland Rd., Lexington, NE 68850
(308) 324-6329, heartlandmuseum.com

67

MEET ARCHIE AND FRIENDS

AT MORRILL HALL

One of the world's largest mammoth fossils anchors a Nebraska history display. While many will call the early elephant massive, in Nebraska most people call him Archie. Mammoths like Archie could reach a height of more than twelve feet. Archie stars in an exhibit on the main floor of Morrill Hall—a.k.a. the Nebraska State Museum—on the campus of the University of Nebraska–Lincoln. Nebraska was once home to the world's largest prehistoric camel population, so the museum also includes a nine-foot-tall camel fossil. Morrill Hall showcases other prehistoric animals that once roamed the plains in a Smithsonian-quality exhibit. The Cherish Nebraska exhibit stars a saber-toothed tiger and a prehistoric bison, which stood more than seven feet tall with horns that spanned that length.

645 N. Fourteenth St., Lincoln, NE 68588
(402) 472-2637, museum.unl.edu

DID YOU KNOW?

The history of Nebraska's first peoples is recognized in an exhibit at Morrill Hall. First Peoples of the Plains examines the traditions and cultures of the tribes that called the plains home, focusing on their use of natural resources to create tools, clothes, food, and homes.

EXPLORE HISTORY
AT THE MUSEUM OF THE FUR TRADE

Long before cowboys drove herds of cattle across the plains and easterners dreamed of heading west for a new life, a group of men set the stage for American development. Call them mountain men or fur traders, but these people braved frigid Midwestern winters and the sauna of its summers to trap animals and trade or sell their pelts. Located in Chadron, the Museum of the Fur Trade tells its stories through artifacts and memorabilia such as point blankets, including the oldest known blanket, which dates back to 1775. The museum also houses a large weapons collection featuring guns belonging to Kit Carson and Chief Tecumseh. The museum occupies the spot of a former trading post established in 1837. Charles Hanson opened the museum in the mid-1950s, seeking to tell the true stories of fur traders and eschewing the romanticized Hollywood hype.

6321 US Hwy. 20, Chadron, NE 69337
(308) 432-3843, furtrade.org

FUN FACT

James Bordeaux operated the Chadron trading post for the American Fur Company. The trading post, opened in 1837, was a destination for Native American tribes that wintered in the area. Fur trading was a major business in the first half of the 1800s, largely because wealthy men liked to be seen wearing beaver-pelt hats.

BE A GHOSTBUSTER
AT THE MUSEUM OF SHADOWS

Among the restaurants, stores, and offices along Main Street in Plattsmouth sits a unique attraction—the Museum of Shadows. The four-year-old museum attracts both fans of paranormal activity and those who are interested in learning more about the museum's ghostly residents. Occupying four floors of an allegedly haunted building, the Museum of Shadows has earned a solid reputation among paranormal investigators. Voted the most haunted museum in the world, the museum has more than three thousand "verified" haunted artifacts but displays only the safe ones. Items that are deemed to be possessed or dangerous are stored in a secured building. Ayda—a doll with her eyes scratched out that is believed to be attached to the ghost of a six-year-old girl—ranks as the most popular draw. The Museum of Shadows also sponsors ghost hunts, which tend to sell out quickly.

502 Main St., Plattsmouth, NE 68048
(402) 298-4403, museumofshadows.com

FUN FACT

The Cass County Historical Society Museum tells the history of Nebraska's twelfth-largest county, starting in 1854. Among the county's best-known residents was Bess Streeter Aldrich. The Elmwood author gained a reputation as an outstanding writer, publishing novels, articles, and short stories based on family values and Midwestern pioneers. Her home was converted into a museum to share her story.

70

RIDE THE RAILS
AT THE UNION PACIFIC BAILEY YARD

The world's busiest railyard handles about 150 trains daily. Located in North Platte, the Bailey Yard is halfway between Omaha and Denver. It's here where rail cars are switched from one train to another to reach their final destinations in Union Pacific's twenty-three-state region. With seventeen receiving tracks and sixteen outgoing tracks, the Bailey Yard handles about fourteen thousand rail cars in a twenty-four-hour period. Also located onsite is a maintenance building, where technicians address issues with engines' operation. You can watch from the Golden Spike Tower and Visitor Center as trains arrive and rail cars move around the tracks. Open since 2008, the eight-floor tower includes an enclosed observation deck on the top floor and an outdoor viewing area on the seventh floor. A plaza at the base of the tower features the state flags of each state served by Union Pacific.

1249 N. Homestead Rd., North Platte, NE 69101
(308) 532-9920, goldenspiketower.com

North Platte Attractions

Lincoln County Historical Museum

About six million soldiers and sailors traveled through North Platte during World War II, and volunteers served coffee and food to the military guests. That story and a living history town are the highlights of a visit to the Lincoln County Historical Museum.
2403 N. Buffalo Bill Ave., North Platte, NE 69101
(308) 534-5640, lincolncountymuseum.org

North Platte Rail Days

The North Platte Rail Days event celebrates the city's rail history with Bailey Yard tours, food, and games.
(308) 532-9920, northplatteraildays.com

71

LEARN ABOUT AMERICA'S GREATEST SHOWMAN
AT BUFFALO BILL RANCH

Possibly America's first true showman, William F. "Buffalo Bill" Cody wore many hats during his lifetime. Having served as an Army scout, buffalo hunter—where he earned his nickname after killing nearly seventy buffalo in one day—and Pony Express rider, he turned to show business after his "retirement." He retired to his Scout's Rest Ranch in North Platte, which is now Buffalo Bill Ranch State Historical Park. Buffalo Bill loved to entertain guests at the ranch, which included a stable of horses and wagons. Not far from the ranch, Buffalo Bill had his own cabin, which he used during hunting outings. Anchoring a local rodeo in North Platte, Cody's show became the forerunner of Buffalo Bill's Wild West Show. Buffalo Bill entertained thousands of people around the country and was even invited to have his show performed for the royal family in England.

2921 Scouts Rest Ranch Rd., North Platte, NE 69147
(308) 535-8035, outdoornebraska.gov/buffalobillranch

DID YOU KNOW?

Lakota Sioux chief Sitting Bull was a member of Buffalo Bill's Wild West Show. They developed a friendship that lasted beyond Chief Sitting Bull's time with the show.

North Platte Attractions

Cody Park

This park is home to a small zoo, carousel, and train yard. A Buffalo Bill Cody memorial greets park visitors at the entrance.
1400 N. Jeffers St., North Platte, NE 69101
(308) 535-6700, ci.north-platte.ne.us/parks/cody-park

Fort Cody Trading Post

A perfect spot to buy souvenirs. The trading post is home to a miniature display of a wild west show. The shop has several unique items to check out, including a stuffed two-headed calf.
221 Halligan Dr., North Platte, NE 69101
(308) 532-8081, fortcody.com

Fort McPherson National Cemetery

Honoring America's fallen soldiers, Fort McPherson is the final resting place for military members and veterans dating back to the American Indian Wars. The headstones are aligned in perfect symmetry, and visitors are encouraged to honor the men and women who rest here eternally.
12004 S. Spur 56A, Maxwell, NE 69151
(308) 582-4433, nps.gov/nr/travel/national_cemeteries/Nebraska/Fort_McPherson_National_Cemetery.html

Twentieth Century Veterans Memorial

Located just south of town off I-80, this memorial honors veterans from each military branch and World War II canteen volunteers.
2811 S. Jeffers St., North Platte, NE 69103
(308) 532-6579, visitnorthplatte.com/directory-posts/20th-century-veterans-memorial

Grain Bin Antique Town

Built within wooden storage bins from the Depression era, this antiques market is the perfect place to search for eclectic items, such as antique furniture and vintage clothing. It's located in the rolling hills a few miles outside of North Platte.
10641 S. Old Hwy. 83, North Platte, NE 69101
(308) 539-7401, grainbinantiquetown.com

RELIVE HISTORY
AT OMAHA'S OLD MARKET

With brick streets and cast-iron storefronts, Omaha's Old Market harks back to the days of horse-drawn wagons, when merchants sold their wares along the street. Today you can relive that scene at the seasonal farmers' market, where vendors sell clothing, fruit, and vegetables along the same streets. While it's fun to reflect on its history, the Old Market continues to grow as a retail and entertainment area. Restaurants, stores, art galleries, museums, and condominiums now call century-old buildings home. The Old Market is on the National Register of Historic Places, and you'll see faded signs—ghost ads—painted on the sides of buildings. During the day, families and couples roam the nine-square-block area, searching for a good meal and shopping deals. At night the Old Market takes on a new life, with couples enjoying date nights and a younger crowd hitting the clubs and bars for an evening of revelry.

oldmarket.com

DID YOU KNOW?

The late Mark Mercer is credited with saving the Old Market from destruction in the 1960s. His leadership led to the development of the area, which covers nine square blocks from Tenth and Farnam to Thirteenth and Jackson streets. It has since grown into one of the most popular areas in Omaha.

APPRECIATE WESTERN ART
AT THE PETRIFIED WOOD GALLERY

Howard and Harvey Kenfield started by collecting Native American arrowheads as children. Then the twins turned their attention to making art out of petrified wood they found in the area. Word soon spread about their unique sculptures, which depict cabins, barns, and other Western themes. Today the Kenfield twins' hobby attracts visitors from around the world to the Petrified Wood Gallery in Ogallala. The gallery hosts special exhibitions, such as pieces from the Petrified Forest in Arizona and the Stone Forest in China. While petrified wood may have taken over the Kenfields' adulthood, the gallery also showcases the twins' childhood love of arrowheads with an exhibit that includes several discovered near Ogallala. The gallery also has pewter and marble sculptures and figurines that help tell the story of the West.

418 E. First St., Ogallala, NE 69153
(308) 284-9996, petrifiedwoodgallery.com

FUN FACT

Ogallala is known as the Cowboy Capital of Nebraska because it marked the end of the trail for Texas cattle drives in the late 1800s. Today, that story is told with steak and a show. Front Street Steakhouse and Crystal Palace Saloon anchor the city's Front Street attraction, which resembles an 1800s-era town.

CELEBRATE AMERICA'S PROGRESS
AT PIONEER VILLAGE

Telling the story of America's progress from the mid-1800s to the 1960s (and a few years beyond), Harold Warp's Pioneer Village remains a staple of rural Nebraska attractions. With nearly thirty buildings spread over twenty acres, the living history museum resembles an 1800s western town, including a fort, one-room schoolhouse, church, and sod house. As you stroll through sixteen other buildings housing exhibits, you'll notice that each traces a theme, such as automobiles or farm equipment, chronologically. While Pioneer Village tells the story of American progress from a national perspective, it also highlights local history, such as a replica of US Senator Carl Curtis's office. Oddly, the museum also includes an exhibit on computers from the 1980s. Who knows? Maybe Pioneer Village will open a section on progress from the 1970s through today.

138 E. US Hwy. 6, Minden, NE 68959
(308) 832-1181, pioneervillage.org

DID YOU KNOW?

Minden is Nebraska's Christmas City. Lights are strung from the dome of the Kearney County courthouse, and each window is decorated in alternating green and red lights. The display includes more than twelve thousand bulbs, and they can be seen for miles.

SEW UP A VISIT
TO THE INTERNATIONAL QUILT MUSEUM

As soon as you see *Reverie*, with its beautiful strands of ribbon-like white metal, in front of the International Quilt Museum, you know you're in for a special visit. Even the building's modern design adds to expectations. You may think you're going to see quilts like the ones at your grandma's house, but you're in for a shock. The International Quilt Museum showcases true works of art, with beautifully designed quilts from around the world dating from the 1700s through today. The museum features more than six thousand quilts, each with its own unique style and story. Opened in 1997 following a donation of nearly one thousand quilts, the International Quilt Museum is now considered the home of quilting experts. With the ongoing popularity of quilting, the museum strives to create a collection that recognizes the cultural and artistic importance of quilts around the world.

1523 N. Thirty-Third St., Lincoln, NE 68583
(402) 472-6549, internationalquiltmuseum.org

76

ATTEND
A POWWOW

Nebraska's four major tribes celebrate their heritage and culture annually with powwows. Attending a powwow is an excellent opportunity to learn about a tribe's history and some of its traditions. Of the four tribes, the Omaha (Umo^{n}ho^{n}) and Ponca (Pá^{n}ka) hail from Nebraska. The federal government relocated the Santee Sioux (Isanti) and Winnebago (Ho Chunk) from Minnesota and Wisconsin, respectively. Santee actually hosts a *wacipi* (Dakota/Sioux for powwow). Powwow emcees provide humor as they explain the significance of the songs and dances, including traditional and fancy styles such as shawl, grass, and jingle. Each powwow begins with the Grand Entry into the arena. Always following a circle, dancers enter behind veterans carrying the American flag, military flags, and the eagle staff, which is held in high esteem by each tribe.

Nebraska Powwows

Santee Sioux Tribe (Third weekend of June)
108 Spirit Lake Ave. W., Niobrara, NE 68760
(402) 857-2772, santeesiouxnation.net

Winnebago Tribe (Last weekend of July)
Veterans Memorial Park, East Avenue, Winnebago, NE 68071
(402) 878-2272, winnebagotribe.com

Ponca Tribe (Second weekend of August)
2523 Woodbine St., Niobrara, NE 68760
(402) 857-3391, poncatribe-ne.org

Omaha Tribe (Mid-August)
Macy, NE 68039
(402) 837-5391, facebook.com/omahatribeofnebraska

Wambli Sapa Memorial Powwow at UNO (First weekend of April)
6001 Dodge St., Omaha, NE 68182
(402) 554-2829, unomaha.edu/college-of-arts-and-sciences/native-american-studies

Fort Omaha Intertribal Powwow (Third Saturday of September)
5300 N. Thirtieth St., Omaha, NE 68111
(531) 622-2400, mccneb.edu/Prospective-Students/Student-Tools-Resources/Intercultural/Programs-and-Events/Fort-Omaha-Intertribal-Powwow.aspx

UNITE Spring Powwow at UNL (Late April)
222 Nebraska Union, Lincoln, NE 68588
(402) 472-7211, facebook.com/nativeamericansatunl

77

HONOR COLD WAR HEROES
AT THE STRATEGIC AIR COMMAND AND AEROSPACE MUSEUM

Home to the world's largest collection of Cold War-era aircraft, the Strategic Air Command and Aerospace Museum showcases the airpower that helped assert American dominance. A B-1A Lancer bomber greets you at the entrance to the Ashland museum, about a twenty-minute drive from both Omaha and Lincoln on I-80. As if that's not enough, an SR-71 reconnaissance plane welcomes you to the museum's lobby. Then it's all gravy. With nearly three dozen aircraft and seven missiles, the museum offers an in-depth look at Cold War aircraft, including a B-52 bomber and F-4 fighter. While the museum primarily focuses on SAC, which had its headquarters near Omaha, it also features capsules from the space program.

28210 W. Park Hwy., Ashland, NE 68003
(402) 944-3100, sacmuseum.org

DID YOU KNOW?

Clayton Anderson is Nebraska's only astronaut. The Ashland native shares personal memorabilia from his multiple missions to the International Space Station in an exhibit at the SAC and Aerospace Museum.

78

CELEBRATE THE FOURTH
IN SEWARD

Celebrating Independence Day since 1858, Seward was designated Nebraska's official Fourth of July City by state proclamation in 1973. Seward annually attracts thousands of visitors for the holiday. An old-fashioned parade highlights the day's events, with firefighters taking on parade-goers in a water battle. In the end, water balloons always lose against the fire department's water hoses. The parade also includes floats, high school marching bands, and lots of candy being tossed to children lining the streets. While the parade remains the top draw, the day's activities include a craft show, a car show, and lots of food. With its museum located in Seward, the Nebraska National Guard also hosts an exhibit. Then, as the sun sets and darkness falls over the city, the night sky lights up with an impressive fireworks show to cap the day's events.

(402) 643-2928, cityofsewardne.gov

79

WALK IN THE FOOTSTEPS
OF CHIEF STANDING BEAR

Revered among Native Americans, Ponca chief Standing Bear won the first civil rights lawsuit in indigenous history when he sued the federal government in 1879 seeking the right to bury his son on their native land near Niobrara. (In the early 1870s, the government had forced the Ponca to relocate five hundred miles away to a reservation in Oklahoma.) The judge ruled that Native Americans were human and deserved the same rights as others. Recently the state honored Standing Bear with a statue at Centennial Mall in Lincoln, while the Ponca did the same in Niobrara. Today you can walk along the same ground that Chief Standing Bear and his Ponca brothers and sisters traveled during the relocation, as the Ponca tribe recently purchased a stretch of the trail in southeastern Nebraska. About twenty miles long, the path completes a seventy-five-mile walking and bicycling trail between Lincoln and Marysville, Kansas.

(402) 857-3391, chiefstandingbeartrail.com

FUN FACT

Chief Standing Bear was honored with a sculpture in Statuary Hall in the US Capitol in 2019. It was a major honor for the Ponca tribe, as well as other Nebraska tribes.

80

VISIT
THE STRAW BALE CHURCH

In the early days, with building materials often difficult to come by or too expensive, Nebraskans made do with local resources. What did most farms have plenty of? Hay. So Nebraskans turned to hay or straw for construction needs. In Arthur, locals used straw bales to build a church, plastering it both inside and out. It was constructed in 1928, about sixteen years before the town was incorporated. The community developed as a result of the Kinkaid Act, which encouraged settlement in Nebraska's panhandle. Today the Pilgrim Holiness Church may not hold regular services, but it's open for self-guided tours (donations requested). Named to the National Register of Historic Places in 1979, it ranks as the oldest straw bale church in North America.

216 Cedar St., Arthur, NE 69121
(308) 764-2362, facebook.com/pages/Pilgrim-Holiness-Church-Arthur-Nebraska

LEARN ABOUT NEBRASKA'S POPULISM HISTORY

AT STATE CAPITOL

Populism describes the history of Nebraska's state government. From William Jennings Bryan to George Norris, Nebraska politicians have long portrayed themselves as being of the people, the state's electorate. The state is known nationally for its unicameral (one-house) legislature, where forty-nine state senators serve as non-partisan representatives of their districts. Because of term limits, senators serve a maximum of two four-year terms. The governor and other state officials also work at the Capitol. A skyscraper, the building is one of only four state capitols built in this style. Visitors are welcome to tour the Capitol, which displays artwork representing the state's history. On the second floor, busts recognize Nebraskans named to the Nebraska Hall of Fame, including Ponca chief Standing Bear, General John J. Pershing, and author Mari Sandoz. The fourteenth floor houses an observation deck and showcases the state's history through a series of murals.

1445 K St., Lincoln, NE 68508
(402) 471-0448, capitol.nebraska.gov

DID YOU KNOW?

Lincoln's appointment as the state capital came with controversy. An Omaha faction wanted the capital to remain in Omaha, as it had served as the territorial capital. Besides suggesting the capital be located in a fictional town, Lincoln opponents suggested renaming Lancaster to Lincoln after President Abraham Lincoln to appeal to Confederate supporters who would oppose the name change. The idea failed, but Lancaster was renamed Lincoln anyway. The city has served as the state capital since Nebraska became a state in 1867.

Lincoln Attractions

Nebraska History Museum

With several cultures settling in Nebraska, the Nebraska History Museum covers about twelve thousand years of state history. From Native Americans to European settlers, the museum explores the state through special exhibits about the women's suffrage movement and auto racing.

131 Centennial Mall N., Lincoln, NE 68508

(402) 471-4782, history.nebraska.gov/museum

Sheldon Museum of Art

With more than thirteen thousand pieces of art in its collection, the Sheldon Museum of Art on the campus of the University of Nebraska–Lincoln showcases American art ranging from nineteenth century landscapes to expressionism.

Twelfth and R streets, Lincoln, NE 68508

(402) 472-2461, sheldonartmuseum.org

Great Plains Art Museum

Focusing on Western art from the Great Plains, this museum houses a collection featuring artists such as Frederic Remington and Charles Russell. Exhibits are regularly rotated, so visit often.

1155 Q St., Lincoln, NE 68588

(402) 472-6220, unl.edu/plains/great-plains-art-museum

Larsen Tractor Test & Power Museum

Home to classic tractors, the Larsen Tractor Test & Power Museum was once used for testing farm equipment.

1925 N. Thirty-Seventh St., Lincoln, NE 68503

(402) 472-8389, tractormuseum.unl.edu

BECOME A WILLA CATHER CHARACTER
IN RED CLOUD

Pulitzer Prize–winning author Willa Cather based many of her books' characters on people she knew in Red Cloud. Although born in Virginia, Cather and her family moved to Red Cloud during her childhood, and she considered Red Cloud her hometown. Cather used locals as inspiration for novels such as *O Pioneers!*, *My Ántonia*, *The Song of the Lark*, and *Lucy Gayheart*. Cather enthusiasts enjoy visiting her childhood home, which has been named to the National Register of Historic Places. You can see her room as it may have appeared while she lived there. You can also spend the night at the second Cather home, which is now a bed and breakfast. The National Willa Cather Center in Red Cloud celebrates Cather's story with a museum and archives, as well as special exhibits and tours that showcase the homes and buildings used as inspiration for her stories.

National Willa Cather Center, 413 N. Webster St., Red Cloud, NE 68970
(402) 746-2653, willacather.org

DID YOU KNOW?

Willa Cather worked as a reporter and editor in Pittsburgh before becoming a novelist. She wrote twelve books, half of them based on life on the prairie.

Red Cloud Attractions

Red Cloud Opera House

Built in 1885, the Opera House hosted many musical programs and civic functions, including Willa Cather's high school graduation. The Opera House has seen renewed life with concerts hosted on a regular basis.
411 N. Webster St., Red Cloud, NE 68970
(402) 746-2653, willacather.org/opera-house-events

Republican River

Perfect for wildlife viewing, the Republican River is ripe for seeing eagles, deer, birds, and even bobcats. A great spot for water activities, such as fishing, the area has beautiful scenery with cliffs and rolling hills.
US Highway 81 and River Road, Red Cloud, NE 68970

Starke Round Barn

Nearly 120 years old, the Starke Round Barn is the largest round barn in Nebraska—and one of the largest in the country—at about 130 feet in diameter and three stories tall. The Starke family used the top level to store hay. The main level housed farm machinery, while the lower level was for livestock. The barn is open for tours and special events.
1639 US Hwy. 136, Red Cloud, NE 68970
(402) 746-4165, facebook.com/StarkeRoundBarnNebraska/?ref=br_rs

CHOOSE A FAVORITE SON
AT WAHOO'S MUSEUM

It's rare for a small, rural town to turn out one famous person, let alone five. But five famous men hail from Wahoo. The Saunders County Historical Society and Museum celebrates their accomplishments while also offering other interesting exhibits. Possibly the best known of the group, movie mogul Darryl Zanuck founded Twentieth Century-Fox Film Corporation and produced nearly 250 movies, including *The Grapes of Wrath* and *The Longest Day*. Howard Hanson won the Pulitzer Prize as a music composer. An inductee into the Baseball Hall of Fame, Sam Crawford enjoyed a nineteen-year Major League Baseball career. While he served as president of the University of Chicago, George Beadle was also honored as a Nobel recipient in physiology. As the fifth member of this elite group, C. W. Anderson authored more than thirty children's books while also creating covers for the *Saturday Evening Post*.

240 N. Walnut St., Wahoo, NE 68066
(402) 443-3090, saunderscomuseum.org

DID YOU KNOW?

On the *Late Show*, David Letterman sometimes identified cities and towns as the "home office" and source of the popular Top 10 list. Wahoo enjoyed the spotlight as the home office for several episodes. Wahoo leaders took advantage of the attention, using a telephone booth as the "office."

VÄLKOMMEN TILL OAKLAND,

EXPLORE NEBRASKA'S SWEDISH CAPITAL

Ask someone where the Swedish Capital of Nebraska is and you'll likely start a major debate. While other towns may claim they're the capital, both a governor and a Swedish consul-general have declared Oakland the official Swedish capital of Nebraska. A visit to the Swedish Heritage Center, located inside a converted church, tops a trip to Oakland; you'll explore the city's Scandinavian influence and learn about Sweden's provinces. From Oakland's early train depot to the Oakland High School Vikings, you'll get a true glimpse into life in the town founded by John Oak. Following your visit to the Swedish Heritage Center, head to Oakland Avenue and stroll downtown, taking in the beauty of vintage buildings.

301 N. Charde Ave., Oakland, NE 68045
(402) 380-9744, swedishheritagecenter.org

NEBRASKA'S SWEDE CAPITAL

Stromsburg also lays claim as Nebraska's Swedish capital. However, its designation differs from Oakland in that it was named as the Swede capital by Gov. Frank Morrison, rather than the Swedish capital. Stromsburg boasts a strong Scandinavian ancestry, with about 30 percent of its population claiming Swedish heritage. The city celebrates its heritage each June with the Swedish Festival, including a parade, food, and music.

85

TRAVEL BACK IN TIME
AT THE STUHR MUSEUM

Stroll down memory lane and explore early life in Central Nebraska, from the days of Native Americans to the arrival of white settlers. The Stuhr Museum of the Prairie Pioneer in Grand Island highlights local life from the 1800s through the mid-1900s. Take a selfie in front of a vintage windmill as you explore displays of Native American life and tools, as well as Old West horses. The museum itself is an architectural marvel. Designed by the same architect who created the Kennedy Center for the Performing Arts, the building has a sleek appearance, a spiral staircase, and attractive water fountains. Outside, the museum complex includes an old rail town with reenactors, such as a blacksmith. Stroll through the western town and imagine what life was like in the late 1800s in rural Nebraska. A Pawnee tribal earth lodge adds to the Stuhr's historical look.

3133 W. Hwy. 34, Grand Island, NE 68801
(308) 385-5316, stuhrmuseum.org

DID YOU KNOW?

Oscar-winning actor Henry Fonda hailed from Grand Island. The actor's childhood home is one of the residences displayed at the Stuhr Museum's living history rail town. Fonda started his acting career in Omaha on the recommendation of the mother of another Nebraska native and Academy Award winner, Marlon Brando.

Grand Island Attractions

Fonner Park

Home to thoroughbred horseracing in the spring and the state fair in the summer, Fonner Park is a venerable facility with a great history.
700 E. Stolley Park Rd., Grand Island, NE 68802
(308) 382-4515, fonnerpark.com

Wave Pizza Co.

While it serves outstanding pizza and wings, Wave Pizza Co. is also a must-see for its atmosphere. Home to beach-themed attractions, including the salt shaker Jimmy Buffett allegedly sings about in "Margaritaville," Wave Pizza Co. is an experience.
107 N. Walnut St., Grand Island, NE 68801
(308) 308 -9283, wavepizzaco.com

Fred's Flying Circus

Flying high above a Grand Island auto repair shop, Fred's Flying Circus offers a menagerie of auto art with cartoon characters riding in cars created by the late Fred Schritt. With Fred driving a Coney Car, Shrek steering a taxi, and the Red Baron flying his plane, passersby are enthralled by the unique art.
503 E. Fourth St., Grand Island, NE 68801
(308) 384-8808, facebook.com/gibodyshop

Raising Nebraska

A tribute to the importance of agriculture in the state, Raising Nebraska offers an opportunity to learn about farming and its role in everyday life.

Nebraska State Fairgrounds

501 E. Fonner Park Rd., Grand Island, NE 68801
(308) 385-3967, raisingnebraska.unl.edu

DIG FOR FOSSILS
AT ASHFALL FOSSIL BEDS STATE HISTORICAL PARK

From miniature horses to camels and small rhinos, many prehistoric animals roamed the northeast Nebraska countryside. Then, one day, it all ended. The skies darkened with ash from a volcanic eruption hundreds of miles away in Utah. Within days, all the animals that had once lived in the idyllic grasslands were gone. About twelve million years later, a paleontologist discovered the first set of fossils here, the remains of a baby rhinoceros. As more and more fossils were discovered—even a saber-toothed deer—the site near Royal became a tourist attraction. Thousands of people visit Ashfall Fossil Beds State Historical Park each year during the dig season where they walk along a boardwalk and view actual fossils that remain embedded in the ground.

86930 517th Ave., Royal, NE 68773
(402) 893-2000, ashfall.unl.edu

DID YOU KNOW?

Long before its grasslands days, Nebraska was part of a prehistoric tropical sea. The plesiosaur was among the water's largest predators. The oldest set of fossils found for the creature was discovered on the Santee Sioux reservation, about an hour from Royal. The remains, believed to be about seventy million years old, are on display at Ashfall Fossils Bed State Park.

5
1

UNIQUE ATTRACTIONS

87

SEE THE WOODEN LOCALS IN TAYLOR

People wave, welcoming you to town. Children walk toward a local fishing hole with fishing rods over their shoulders. There's something amiss about them, though. Say hello to the Taylor Villagers, life-size wooden cutouts designed to attract visitors. The public art project was the brainchild of local artist Marah Sandoz, who thought of the idea after attending an economic development meeting. The black-and-white figures represent people who may have lived in Taylor in the early 1900s, when the town was at its peak with nearly four hundred residents. More than a hundred wooden villagers are located around town, and the artist has added about six new characters annually since 2003. As you walk around town meeting Taylor's wooden villagers, stop by any of the local shops and meet the real villagers, all 190 of them.

Highways 183 and 91, Taylor, NE 68874
(308) 214-0847, visitnebraska.com/taylor/taylor-villagers

88

VISIT THE PLAINS' MILE MARKER
AT CHIMNEY ROCK

Chimney Rock in western Nebraska stood as a beacon for pioneers traveling west during the mid-1800s. Pioneers on the Oregon, California, and Mormon trails used the rock formation to mark their travel through the plains. As you approach Chimney Rock, your eyes will widen in amazement at the beauty of the rock formation standing tall in the panhandle. Native Americans referred to Chimney Rock with names such as teepee and wigwam. Likely given its current name by early fur traders, today Chimney Rock National Historic Site serves as the most recognizable attraction in Nebraska. Located about four miles from Bayard, the three-hundred-foot-tall geological wonder is a major tourist attraction. The visitors center offers museum exhibits and trail maps, as well as media programs.

9822 County Road 75 and Highway 92, Bayard, NE 69334
(308) 586-2581, visitscottsbluff.com/attraction/chimney-rock-national-historic-site

DID YOU KNOW?

Chimney Rock suffers erosion almost yearly because of weather-related events such as storms and lightning.

WING IN
TO VIEW THE SANDHILL CRANE MIGRATION

More than half a million sandhill cranes visit Nebraska over a six-week period from late February to early April as part of an annual northern migration dating back millions of years. The cranes spend time along the Platte River valley in the Central Flyway, which runs about one hundred miles from Grand Island to North Platte. Kearney serves as the central location for the migration, attracting the majority of tourists and bird enthusiasts who visit from almost every state and more than sixty countries. People participate in tours to blinds or observation decks along the river to watch the birds take off in the morning and return at night.

The sandhill cranes are majestic birds, standing three to four feet tall. They are gray with a patch of red on their foreheads. Their bugle call is among the most unique sounds you'll hear in nature. The birds spend days eating corn, seeds, and bugs in unplowed farm fields. At night, they group together on sandbars in the Platte River, which provide protection from predators such as coyotes, foxes, and bobcats.

DID YOU KNOW?

As you travel the countryside viewing sandhill cranes, you may be one of a fortunate few to see the endangered whooping crane alongside them. Only a handful of whooping cranes exist, and they often fly with the Sandhill cranes during their northern migration.

Kearney Visitors Bureau
1007 Second Ave., Kearney, NE 68847
(308) 237-3178, visitkearney.org

Iain Nicolson Audubon Center at Rowe Sanctuary
44450 Elm Island Rd., Gibbon, NE 68840
(308) 468-5282, rowe.audubon.org

Crane Trust (Grand Island area)
9325 S. Alda Rd., Wood River, NE 68883
(308) 382-1820, cranetrust.org

North Platte/Lincoln County Visitors Bureau
101 Halligan Dr., North Platte, NE 69101
(308) 532-4729, visitnorthplatte.com

CHECK IN
AT THE HISTORIC ARGO HOTEL

It's been said that spirits haunt the Historic Argo Hotel in Crofton. While the appeal of roaming ghosts attracts some visitors, the inn also offers an opportunity to stay in a hotel with ties to Nebraska's railroad history. Built in the early twentieth century to meet the needs of rail travelers, the Crofton hotel has experienced an interesting life. A few years after opening as the Hotel Argo, its owners sold it, and the name changed to the New Meridian Hotel. In the mid-1930s, it became a health clinic. Later, when a physician's office closed here, the building stood vacant until it reopened in 1994 as the Historic Argo Hotel. Named to the National Register of Historic Places, the hotel offers eleven guest rooms on the second floor. Oh, and the ghosts don't seem to mind the visitors.

211 W. Kansas St., Crofton, NE 68730
(402) 388-2400, facebook.com/TheHistoricalArgoHotel

FUN FACT

A future Hollywood starlet called the hotel home during the summer months in the early 1930s. Leslie Brooks—born Virginia Leslie Gettman—spent a couple of summers in Crofton when her grandparents ran the hotel. The actress performed in thirty movies during her career.

RIDE THE WAVES
ON A SANDHILLS DRIVE

With their sandy rolling hills and flowing prairie grasses and other native plants, the Nebraska Sandhills serve as a reminder that this was once a prehistoric sea. A drive through the seemingly endless waves of grass provides a relaxing experience. The nearly 275-mile-long Sandhills Journey Scenic Byway takes you from Grand Island to Alliance. Along the way, you'll find attractions such as the Nebraska National Forest near Halsey, with about ninety thousand acres. While you're there, visit the Scott Lookout Tower, where you can climb fifty feet to the top observation deck. Built in the mid-1900s to serve as a fire lookout, the Scott Lookout Tower is still used by rangers when there is a risk of wildfires. Calling Alliance home, Carhenge uses old cars painted gray to create a replica of the famous Stonehenge.

(308) 546-0636, sandhillsjourney.com

FUN FACT

You can still find wagon ruts from the Oregon and Mormon trails in Sandhills fields.

MINE FOR CHALK
AT HAPPY JACK IN SCOTIA

Don't mistake the Happy Jack Chalk Mine for a cave. Nebraska, formerly a prehistoric sea, was mined for chalk from the 1870s through the mid-1900s. But the "chalk" was actually diatomite, a phytoplankton that lived more than a million years ago. As the climate changed, the diatomite fossils found inside the mine turned into chalk. You can still find fossils in the mine's walls. Happy Jack Chalk Mine got its name from an old trader, "Happy Jack" Swearengen, who once greeted people settling the area. After the mine closed, the state filled in several rooms with debris. But Happy Jack reopened to the public in 1997. After visiting the mine, climb Happy Jack Peak, which offers an impressive view of the Loup River Valley.

80131 NE Hwy. 11, Scotia, NE 68875
(308) 245-3276, happyjackchalkmine.org

DID YOU KNOW?

Nebraska is one of the world's popcorn capitals, producing about 25 percent of the nation's supply. North Loup, about five miles from Scotia, celebrates the state's cash crop with Popcorn Days every August. Featuring a parade, carnival rides, and other fun and games—and, of course, popcorn—Popcorn Days is a fun family festival.

93

PAY YOUR RESPECTS
AT HOLY FAMILY SHRINE

An architectural gem, this little chapel stands high atop a hill overlooking the Platte River valley as motorists travel along I-80. Located about twenty-five miles west of Omaha near Gretna, the glass-enclosed Holy Family Shrine welcomes visitors who are seeking a spiritual connection or who are just intrigued by its beauty. With wood arches resembling prairie grass waving in the wind, the chapel's glass walls reach nearly fifty feet tall. While the interior invites people to appreciate its beauty, officials encourage visitors to spend time praying, meditating, or reflecting. The shrine doesn't have an assigned priest or daily services, but a priest conducts mass here each Saturday morning. Outside, flowers and plants add to the beauty of the chapel. With about thirty thousand visitors annually, the visitor center also traces the shrine's history.

23132 Pflug Rd., Gretna, NE 68028
(402) 332-4565, holyfamilyshrineproject.com

94

LAUGH
AT THE KLOWN DOLL MUSEUM

You may not want to break into a version of "Send in the Clowns" when you visit the Klown Doll Museum—you never know what might happen. With more than seven thousand clown dolls, paintings, and figurines calling a former gas station and café home, the world's largest clown collection resides in Plainview. It started as an innocent act of putting a few clown dolls on a window ledge at the local chamber of commerce. Soon after, people started dropping off clown figures, mugs, and other collectibles, which became the collection of the Klown Doll Museum. Then donations started coming from outside of town. With seven major collections, some donations included more than twelve hundred items. Among the exhibits you'll find figurines that celebrate the careers of famous clowns, such as Emmett Kelly. The museum also has five replicas of paintings by famed entertainer Red Skelton.

306 W. Park Ave., Plainview, NE 68769
(402) 582-4433, klowndollmuseum.com

FUN FACT

The "K" in Klown Doll Museum comes from the community's band. More than fifty years ago, band organizers thought it would be cute to spell clown with a "K."

95

VISIT THE LIGHTHOUSE WITHOUT A LIGHT
AT LAKE MINATARE

Rising high above the trees, this lighthouse seemingly stands guard along the shoreline, ready to guide weary boaters on Lake Minatare. Only there's a slight catch—there's no light in the lighthouse. Built in 1939, the stone lighthouse actually serves as a shelter and observation tower. Resembling a lighthouse you'd likely find on the east or west coasts, the tower stands fifty-five feet high. You can always pretend you're a lighthouse caretaker and climb the narrow steps to the top, where you can appreciate a beautiful view of Lake Minatare. The lake, the largest in the panhandle, features about twenty-three hundred acres of water, perfect for boating, swimming, and camping. Water skiing is another fun activity you'll find on the water. Wildlife enthusiasts will find many opportunities to view waterfowl and migratory birds because the state recreation area is part of the North Platte National Wildlife Refuge.

Minatare, NE 69356
(308) 783-2911, outdoornebraska.gov/lakeminatare

FIND YOUR WAY AT SCOTTS BLUFF NATIONAL MONUMENT

Serving as the GPS of the 1800s, Scotts Bluff marked the end of prairie travel and the start of more rigorous mountain trails for pioneers along the Oregon and California trails. Today, the Scotts Bluff National Monument protects about three thousand acres of prairie grass, as well as parts of the trails. On four miles of hiking trails, visitors actually walk the same path that settlers did. You can also drive to the top of the monument. It rises eight hundred feet above the prairie, so you may want to bring a basket and enjoy a picnic at the site, where you can see about ninety miles in any direction, taking in Chimney Rock and scenery from other states. Scotts Bluff has been a national monument since 1919, and park rangers dress as fur traders and pioneers to provide authenticity as they host discussions about the people who passed through.

190276 Old Oregon Trail, Gering, NE 69341
(308) 436-9700, nps.gov/scbl

Scottsbluff Attractions

Riverside Discovery Center

With nearly two hundred animals, including almost twenty endangered species, this twenty-two-acre zoo offers a unique experience. The zoo also has a petting zoo and children's play area.

1600 S. Beltline Hwy. W., Scottsbluff, NE 69361

(308) 630-6236, riversidediscoverycenter.org

Robidoux Pass National Historic Landmark and Trading Post

A trading spot for Native Americans, this trading post also offered respite for settlers traveling west. Today the national historic site includes wagon ruts and pioneer graves.

Highway 71, Gering, NE 69341

(308) 436-6886, nps.gov/nr/travel/scotts_bluff/robidoux_pass.html

Victory Hill Farm

A family-owned farm that specializes in goat cheese.

200444 County Rd. F, Scottsbluff, NE 69361

(308) 630-0530, facebook.com/Victory-Hill-Farm-571908262821450

West Nebraska Arts Center

Hosting eighteen exhibitions throughout the year, this arts center focuses on local as well as national artists.

106 E. Eighteenth St., Scottsbluff, NE 69361

(308) 632-2226, thewnac.com

Wildcat Hills State Recreation Area

With more than three miles of trails, this recreation area and nature center offers bird and wildlife viewing year-round. Camping and picnicking are also allowed on site.

210615 Hwy. 71, Gering, NE 69341

(308) 436-3777, outdoornebraska.gov/?s=wildcat+hills

97

FIND OUT WHY VALENTINE IS FOR LOVERS

Known as the Heart City, Valentine in Cherry County proudly shares its name with Valentine's Day. The local post office receives thousands of requests each year to postmark envelopes with VALENTINE on them. As you travel around town, you'll see hearts painted on sidewalks and imprinted on street signs. Named after a congressional representative, Valentine also has the heart of outdoor enthusiasts. The Cowboy Trail—a converted rail line that serves as a bicycle and walking trail—runs through the area, with a quarter-mile bridge that spans the Niobrara River. Fort Niobrara National Wildlife Refuge features bison, elk, and a prairie dog town. While best known for its three-thousand-acre lake with great fishing, boating, and swimming, Merritt Reservoir State Recreation Area embraces the night sky each summer with stargazing parties. The Nebraska Star Party is a week-long celestial event.

Cherry County Tourism and Valentine Visitor's Center
239 S. Main St., Valentine, NE 69201
(402) 376-2969, visitvalentine.org

FUN FACT

The Cowboy Trail runs about two hundred miles from Norfolk to Valentine. Plans call to extend the trail to more than three hundred miles with the addition of Chadron.

Valentine Attractions

Cherry County Historical Society Museum

This museum shares the history of Cherry County, including Native American life and pioneer settlements, and it houses a library with historical records.
249 S. Main St., Valentine, NE 69201
(402) 376-2015, facebook.com/pages/Cherry-County-Historical-Society-Museum/1436029293389883

Centennial Hall Museum

Located inside the oldest surviving high school in Nebraska, the Centennial Hall Museum is a heritage museum offering a look at local history through a series of themed rooms, including a military room and a bell room with more than seventeen hundred bells.
Third and Macomb streets, Valentine, NE 69201
(402) 376-1455, facebook.com/pages/Centennial-Hall/1155847294499465

Valentine National Wildlife Refuge

Home to more than seventy thousand acres of rolling sandhills, this refuge has dozens of lakes and marshes, with many open for fishing. The refuge also allows hunting in select areas. Hiking and other outdoor activities are available for visitors.
39679 Pony Lake Rd., Valentine, NE 69201
(402) 376-3217, fws.gov/refuge/valentine

VISIT MONOWI, AMERICA'S SMALLEST TOWN

Imagine being in charge of street maintenance, clearing snow, and maintaining Main Street's buildings. By yourself. When you're a one-person town, you're responsible for it all. Welcome to Monowi. Population one. As the lone resident of the smallest town in America, Elsie Eiler serves as mayor, town council, and any other necessary role. She also owns Monowi Tavern, which she opened with her husband more than forty years ago. Locals and visitors alike stop in to enjoy a burger and beverage while drinking in the atmosphere. You never know whom you'll meet. People from around the nation and from nearly fifty countries have popped into the tavern. Eiler also manages Rudy Library, a five-thousand-volume collection named after her late husband. While Eiler typically shies away from attention (she is too busy running the tavern and village), Monowi has been featured in national television ads and programs.

Monowi Tavern, 9 Broad St., Monowi, NE 68746
(402) 569-3600, facebook.com/pages/Monowi-Tavern/183099038885583

EXPLORE A NEW WORLD
AT TOADSTOOL GEOLOGIC PARK

You'd swear you were on another planet. It's the precariously balanced rock formations here that give Toadstool Geologic Park its name. With ancient rocks that acquired their appearance over millions of years, Toadstool ranks among the state's most popular attractions and is especially popular with hikers and archaeology enthusiasts. Located in the panhandle, near Crawford, Toadstool Geologic Park's formations stand in the middle of a former riverbed. You can experience the park via a one-mile or three-mile loop. As you explore among the rocks, look for fossils of the animals that once lived in the region. As a nod to the area's history, the US Forest Service has built a sod house using local resources. Commonly referred to as Nebraska's Badlands, Toadstool rivals other natural attractions in the region.

Toadstool Campground, Crawford, NE 69346
(308) 432-0300, fs.usda.gov/recarea/nebraska/recreation/recarea/?recid=10616

EXPLORE QUIRKY
AT CARHENGE

Located just outside Alliance, Carhenge appears to be an homage to the better-known Stonehenge in the United Kingdom. Instead of using centuries-old stone to create his work of art, however, artist Jim Reinders used thirty-eight old cars painted gray to create a copy of the stone formation. Constructed on land that once belonged to the Reinders family, Carhenge is a memorial to the father of the artist, who became intrigued by Stonehenge while studying in the United Kingdom as a college student. He sought to build a different type of memorial to honor his father. After completing Carhenge, the Reinders family donated the land to the city as a public attraction. Carhenge also includes other sculptures using automobiles, such as a fish, a dinosaur, and a "covered wagon," a station wagon featuring a Conestoga wagon frame. It has been voted one of the quirkiest attractions in the United States, and people travel from around the country to visit.

305 Box Butte Ave., Alliance, NE 69301
(308) 762-3569, carhenge.com

SUGGESTED ITINERARIES

HISTORY LESSONS

DATE NIGHT

FAMILY DAY

EXPLORE THE STATE

SPORTS OUTING

EXPLORE THE UNIQUE

ACTIVITIES BY SEASON

SPRING

SUMMER

FALL

WINTER

INDEX